# WEST KOOTENAY
## THE PIONEER YEARS

GARNET BASQUE

SUNFIRE

# SUNFIRE PUBLICATIONS LIMITED

P.O. Box 3399,
Langley, B.C. V3A 4R7

**PRINTING HISTORY**
First Printing — August 1990

**PRODUCTION CREDITS**
Design, layout and maps — Garnet Basque
Typesetting — Kirkrod Printing, Vancouver
Printing — Colorcraft Ltd., Hong Kong

**PHOTO CREDITS**
*All full colour photographs used in this book that are not otherwise credited, were taken by the author.*
B.C. Provincial Archives: 8 (top & bottom), 12 (top), 13 (bottom), 14, 17, 21 (top right & bottom), 28 (top), 29, 31, 36, 38, 39, 42, 46, 47, 51, 54 (top), 55 (right inset), 58 (top), 59 (top right), 62 (top left), 67, 70, 72, 73, 74 (bottom), 75, 79, 82 (centre), 87 (top), 91, 94 (top left & bottom), 98 (top), 99 (top & bottom insets), 102 (top & bottom), 106 (top), 110 (top & bottom), 111 (bottom right), 114 (inset), 118, 119 (top right), 122 (bottom), 130 (top left & bottom), 131 (top), 134 (centre & bottom), 139, 149 (top), 153 (inset), 156 (inset), 157 (left centre & bottom), 161 (top) & 163.
B.C. Government Image Bank: 9, 50 (top & bottom), 86, 98 (bottom), 114 & 134 (top).
Nelson Museum: 43 & 50 (inset).
Ron Inwood: 48-49.
Sunfire Archives: 55 (left inset), 59 (centre), 74 (top), 82 (top three), 155 & 161 (bottom).
Bill Maximick: 83 & 142.
Sandon Historical Society: 115 (bottom).
Vancouver Public Library: 126 (top).
Leah Martin MacKay: 130 (top right).
Canadian Pacific Railway: 143 (top).

**CANADIAN CATALOGUING IN PUBLICATION DATA**

Basque, Garnet.
    West Kootenay : the pioneer years

    Includes bibliographical references.
    ISBN 0-919531-30-X

    1. West Kootenay Region (B.C.)--History.
2. Mines and mineral resources--British
Columbia--West Kootenay Region--History.
I. Title.
FC3845.K7B38 1990        971.1'62        C90-091459-9
F1089.K7B38 1990

Financially assisted by the Ministry of Municipal Affairs, Recreation and Culture through the British Columbia Heritage Trust and British Columbia Lotteries.

# CONTENTS

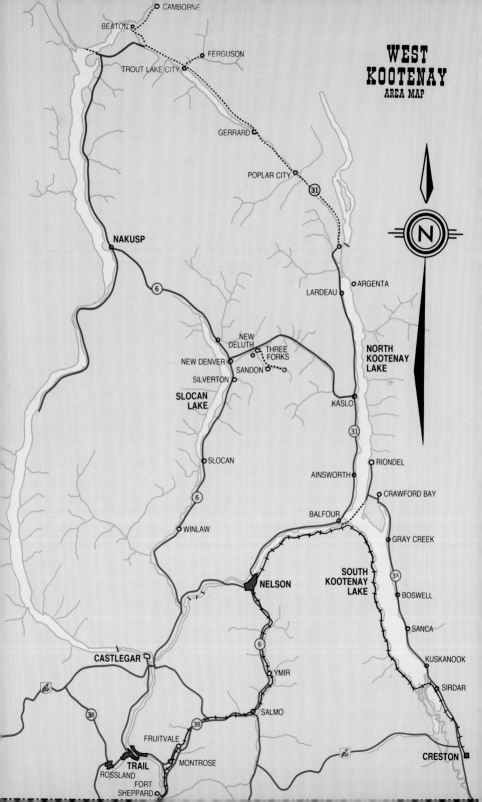

# 1
# BLUEBELL:
# A MINING SAGA

*Many British Columbia mines have fascinating stories of their discovery and development — but none like that of the famous Bluebell on Kootenay Lake.*

TWO well-known pioneers of the Old West contend for the honour of discovering the Bluebell mine. The Scottish botanist, David Douglas, whose surname identifies the Douglas fir tree, and Archibald McDonald, in charge of Fort Colville, now Colville, Washington, from 1833 to 1844. Each has his champions.

Douglas, studying the flora of the Pacific Northwest, explored the upper Columbia River country in the 1820s. He may have seen the rich surface ore on the shores of Kootenay Lake, but the pro-McDonald historians believe otherwise.

". . .still another mineral discovery is credited to Douglas. . ." wrote A.G. Harvey in the *British Columbia Historical Quarterly,* ". . .a great deposit of carbonate lead, galena and copper situate on the east shore of Kootenay Lake. The story. . . .apparently is taken from a report made in 1887 by G.M. Dawson, Director of the Geological Survey of Canada, which states that the ores are said to have been discovered by Douglas in 1825. . . How the story originated is a mystery. . .his carefully written journal makes no mention of it, and, in fact, leaves no room for it."

The Hudson's Bay Company's Archibald McDonald, on the other hand, not only pinpointed the exact site in correspondence (still on file in Beaver House), but one of his letters tells how he sampled "Kootenais treasure" for assay purposes. Unfortunately, the samples and the assays, if they were ever done, have disappeared.

Today, nearly two centuries later, the controversy seems rather academic. The Bluebell mine has closed, probably for the last time, and the community of Riondel faces a future quite different from its recent industrial past.

No matter what happens though, local residents will not forget the colourful history, at least not as long as the Hammill monument stands in camp. Its plaque reads: "Thomas Hammill, assassinated June 1, 1885, age 30 years." Some old-timers, recalling how the young prospectors was working his claim when he was ambushed, say his ghost still haunts the scene.

Be that as it may, the Hammill murder, of which more will be revealed later, was not the first criminal enterprise in Bluebell annals. In the early 1870s an American named Henry Doan went to San Francisco with samples of rich lead-silver ore. He showed them to potential backers, saying he had a mountain of the same ore up in Canada.

He found interested if cautious listeners. The lead was not the main attraction, but significant silver with the lead indicated that the isolated find might be made to pay. Speculators put up a $10,000 bond. Doan received one-tenth in advance, the balance payable after an inspection of the property by a mining expert.

Doan returned to Colville to await the expert. There he asked merchant Ben Bergunder for permission to use a tin shop kept in connection with the Bergunder store.

"I gave him the key," Bergunder recalled in a newspaper interview 40 years later, "and when he returned it to me I noticed his fingers were stained with acid. In a joking manner I asked him if he had been salting ore. He turned red in the face and said no."

Eventually the expert, George Hearst, arrived accompanied by an assayer with full field equipment. Known in mining circles for his shrewdness, he must have worried Doan. Outfitting the party from Bergunder's stock, Hearst hired steamboat captain Pingston as guide, and started out for Kootenay Lake in a small boat manned by six Indians. They struggled upstream on the Columbia River to the mouth of the Kootenay, portaged that stream's turbulent lower reaches, entered the lake and finally landed near the Bluebell outcrop.

The assay equipment landed with them, small thanks to Doan. During the trip he had taken the Indians aside and tried to bribe them to throw it overboard. The chemicals, he explained, were hoodoo and would bring bad luck. How right he was!

Hearst told Bergunder the whole story on his return to Colville. Doan brought the assayer ore samples rich in silver. But Hearst, not liking the "smell" of things, scouted the ground himself and collected more samples. These assayed almost no silver, some lead and considerable zinc, the latter the bugbear of lead metallurgists in those days.

Hearst confronted the hapless Doan and forced a confession. The Bluebell ore was salted; the samples produced in San Francisco had come from Colorado.

Furious, Hearst stripped Doan of money and belongings and told him to get back to Colville as best he might, but alone. The swindler's journey must have been difficult and hazardous, but he did reappear in Colville and was recognized in the Pacific Northwest from time to time until his death at Metaline, Washington, about 1914. George Hearst made a fortune in mining and eventually became a United States Senator. His son, William Randolph, earned fame as the head of the Hearst chain of newspapers.

If the Bluebell gained a bad reputation as the result of Hearst's report, others refused to be discouraged. Small wonder. The shimmering surface ore fascinated all who saw it.

"This rock rises to about 150 feet over the water, and is about three-quarters of a mile long. . ." wrote W.A. Baillie-Grohman in a book published in London, England at the turn of the century concerning his American adventures. "The rusty looking rock was the capping of an extraordinary ledge or vein of argentiferous lead. . . . Further prospecting. . .showed that the vein matter cropped up in parallel streaks almost twenty feet wide along the whole length of the promontory, disclosing a magnitude of deposit which, if it was a continuous one. . .was almost unique in the history of mining. . . .Prospectors thought themselves all ten-fold millionaires, and really, to the eye. . .not without good reason. . . ."

Baillie-Grohman is best remembered for his premature scheme to build an agricultural empire on the flat lands near present-day Creston. But this energetic man also played a key role in events leading up to the bloody Hammill affair which was to make the Bluebell notorious in the west.

Less than 10 years after Doan's attempted swindle, Robert Evan Sproule located and staked the Bluebell promontory. To all intents and purposes, the ore was his.

Sproule was a rough, tough, belligerent American prospector, and one for whom things had never turned out well. He had staked many claims in the United States, including the coal mines at Tacoma, Washington. But even from this big strike he had made little profit.

Then he was attracted to the Kootenay Country, where the "Big Ledge" on the east side of Kootenay Lake had been a legend for 50 years. The outcrop was once so obvious that Indians and trappers smelted lead for bullets from the exposed vein.

In the spring of 1882 Sproule led three men, Hudnut, Myers and Hunley, from Sandpoint, Idaho, in search of the Big Ledge. The expedition was humble, their boat was knocked together at the lake-head and their grubstake was meagre. By this time the ledge was overgrown by forest, but Sproule spotted it easily by tracing the iron streak on the cliffs above it.

The three men each staked claims, the Kootenay Chief, the Comfort and the Ruby, Sproule retaining a large interest in each of them because he was the organizer. The Bluebell claim was staked by Sproule, and so named because of the flowers growing around it.

But the expedition soon turned sour. The men, half-starved because of poor rations, resented being driven by Sproule. Early in the fall, Hudnut, Myers and Hunley took off, stating they would be back with supplies. But their absence was serious. B.C. mining laws stipulated that a miner could not be absent from his claim, without permission from the gold commissioner, from the first of June to the end of October. Sproule, left alone on the dank, shaly beach in front of the Bluebell claim, was uneasy, ill, and felt that he was being watched. He tried to stick it out until October 31, but by October 24 he had only flour left. Sproule was weak and had to get out. He left a note tacked to a Bluebell stake explaining his absence and asserting that he would return in the spring. Then the dejected Sproule rowed southward towards Sandpoint.

He was hardly out of sight before a beautifully appointed boat nosed into Bluebell Bay, and Thomas Hammill and his men landed. Hammill had been closely watching the worsening events in the Sproule camp, and waiting for this moment. Thirty years old, handsome, with a Cornish accent and the manners of an English gentleman, Hammill was financed by the wealthy Capt. George J. Ainsworth of San Francisco, and had lavish equipment and provisions. He was thought by some to be just a "dandy-boy-prospector," but Hammill's credentials were solid — he was a mining engineer, although his ethics were questionable. Hammill declared all the claims on the Bluebell site to be legally abandoned, re-staked them in the names of his men and himself, and settled down to work them.

Sproule, Hudnut, Myers and Hunley returned in the spring of 1883 to find the usurpers firmly entrenched on their claims. Sproule's anger flared almost to the point of violence, but somehow he was persuaded to test his case in court.

On August 31, 1883, court convened in a log cabin on the Bluebell site. Judge Kelly, who was not a judge, but a gold commissioner, presided. Ainsworth hired an expensive lawyer from Victoria to act for Hammill. Both the lawyer and Judge

*(Above) Thomas Hammill, the claim-jumper who was killed by Robert Sproule.*

*(Right) An aerial view of the Bluebell mine and Riondel.*

*(Below) Some early mining activity at the original Bluebell mine site.*

Kelly journeyed to the Kootenays over the dangerously crumbling Dewdney Trail, and both showed the effects of the ordeal. William Baillie-Grohman, who was working on his Creston Flats canal project close by, acted for Sproule. The proceedings lasted seven weeks, mainly because Baillie-Grohman talked incessantly, and so confused Judge Kelly that he missed the point of law completely. He found in favour of Sproule and his colleagues and restored their claims to them.

Hammill, again backed by Ainsworth, took the case to the appeal court in Victoria. It was heard by three judges with Mr. Justice Matthew Begbie rendering the unanimous decision. Judge Begbie found that Hudnut, Myers and Hunley had abandoned their claims during the open season, and legally lost them. But the case of Sproule and the Bluebell claim was different. Sproule had made every effort to stay until the end of the open season and had only been driven out by illness and hunger. So he ruled the Bluebell was legally Sproule's. Begbie also branded Hammill as a professional claim-jumper, as much to be despised as a cattle thief in the Old West.

But, again, Sproule came out of the venture with almost nothing. He had to deed one-third of his interest in the Bluebell to Baillie-Grohman to pay court costs; and Baillie-Grohman, by this time in financial difficulty himself, had — in a final irony — sold his share of the Bluebell to Hammill.

"If that Cornish bastard ever puts a foot or a pick in that claim I will fix him plenty," threatened Sproule. "He will never jump another man's claim."

Charles Molson recalled Sproule's outburst when he heard that Hammill was going to work the Bluebell claim the next day. Sproule had spent the night in Molson's cabin in Ainsworth, across the lake from the Bluebell. When Molson awoke next morning, his guest was gone. He looked out on Kootenay Lake, where the waves were running high, and saw Sproule in his rowboat, battling through the whitecaps towards Bluebell Bay. It was strange because everyone knew that Sproule feared the wide lake when it was rough.

It was 5 a.m. on the fateful morning of June 1, 1885, when Sproule landed safely on the east side of the lake. His men, Charles Wolfe, Adam Wolfe and Charles House, were on the beach, splitting timbers for the mine. They were employed by the Kootenay Mining Company, owned by Doctor Wilbur A. Hendryx and managed by Sproule. The Hendryx interests owned several claims in the area, and most of the Bluebell, but not all of it — through devious manoeuvring Hammill had, as mentioned, acquired a part interest in the Bluebell. The close proximity of Hammill and Sproule was like storing nitroglycerine and gasoline on the same shelf.

Between 9:00 and 10:00 a.m. Sproule asked John Duncan, a Hammill employee, the whereabouts of his boss. There is no record of the answer he received, but a few minutes later Sproule asked Adam Wolfe if he could borrow his gun. Wolfe agreed, reluctantly, but only because Sproule never cleaned it after using it.

A short time later all the men on the beach heard Sproule working in his cabin. Then he emerged and told Charles House to prepare lunch. He also announced, suddenly, that he had to leave the camp unexpectedly, but would return that night or the next day. Sproule then loaded his boat with his own gun, some provisions and his oilskin coat. The three workmen agreed that Sproule appeared to be angry and flustered as he rowed away.

Adam Wolfe found his gun had been returned to his cabin uncleaned, as usual, with a spent cartridge in the chamber. He kept the cartridge because, he later testified, he was sure, from that moment, that something was wrong. In Wolfe's cabin the men also found a note from Sproule saying he might be gone for some time, ordering them to continue working, and assuring them that their wages would be paid.

None of the men were aware of the drama which had taken place only a few hundred yards from them. Hammill had been working the Bluebell claim that morning. Nick Belnouf was working out of sight, but within sound of him. About 11 o'clock, both Belnouf and John Duncan, who was also working nearby, heard a shot, but neither thought it important: the miners were always shooting game.

On his way to the Hammill cabin at noon, Belnouf found a man on the path, so blood-smeared and contorted by pain that at first he did not recognize him. It was Hammill. Belnouf ran for help, and he and Duncan carried the wounded man to his cabin. They found that a bullet had splintered Hammill's spine, which made his death agonizing. Hammill died within an hour without identifying his assailant, whom he probably never saw.

Const. Henry Anderson was summoned from Ainsworth and arrived at the Bluebell mine about 2 p.m. In his report of the day, Anderson said that the men at the site swamped him with a barrage of misleading and contradictory statements. Sproule's men first declared that he had left the camp between seven and 10 in the morning, then remembered that it had been after 11 — or so they thought. The letter from Sproule was not mentioned until much later. In the first interview the Wolfes and House assured Anderson that Sproule had just gone over to Ainsworth.

Anderson hurriedly returned to Ainsworth, but of course did not find Sproule. A posse, organized and headed by Anderson, rowed furiously south towards the international boundary. Three days later, early in the morning and very close to the border, Sproule walked out of the bush and into the camp of his pursuers.

These were the events which led to the trial of Sproule for the murder of Hammill in Victoria on December 7, 1885, with the Hon. John Hamilton Gray presiding judge. The prosecution pressed vehemently for conviction. The judge told the jury that if they convicted according to their consciences, without a shadow of doubt in their minds as to the prisoner's guilt, even if the verdict was proved by later events to have been incorrect, they would still be justified before God and man for what they had done. This seems a strange perversion of the hallowed concept in British justice that a man shall not be convicted if there is one shred of doubt as to his guilt.

In his summation the defence lawyer pointed out the many holes in the case. On the morning of June 1, Sproule was actually using a trolling line when he left the Bluebell, which did not suggest a sudden, desperate attempt to escape. Furthermore, it was quite usual for Sproule to make unexpected and unexplained trips to Sandpoint. The threat by Sproule to "fix" Hammill was not raised in the resume; presumably the defense considered that it was obvious that Sproule, with his quick temper, might make such a threat, but not follow it through. The defence concentrated on the contradictory statements of the Crown's star witnesses, the two Wolfe brothers, and attempted to show that their testimony proved absolutely nothing.

In his address to the jury, Mr. Justice Gray, while admitting the evidence was, in his own words, "certainly of the most unusual and extraordinary character," then went on to say, "I cannot define any other theory by which the crime could have happened than that adduced by the Crown."

The jury retired at 4:40 in the afternoon, asked once for more instruction from the judge, then, at 11 o'clock the next morning, returned their verdict. They found

*(Opposite page, top) The Bluebell mine in 1898.*

*(Opposite page, bottom left) A solitary fire hydrant sits on the vacated, fenced-in, Bluebell mine site. In the background is the tunnel which was started in 1950.*

*(Opposite page, bottom right) The remains of the Bluebell mine's head frame and cages in May, 1985. The mines were ordered closed by COMINCO on December 21, 1971, and the buildings were demolished in 1973.*

*(Right) B.C. Government Point-of-Interest plaque near Riondel.*

*(Below) The Kootenay Mining & Smelting Company's smelter at Pilot Bay in 1896. Today, only the two brick chimneys remain on the site.*

BLUE BELL MINE

The orebody, known to Indians as a source of lead for musket balls, was staked in 1882 by Bob Sproule, later restaked by Tom Hamill. The resulting lawsuit cost Sproule the property, and in revenge he murdered his rival; was convicted and hanged. Development included a smelter and a townsite. This mine has the longest history in the province.

PROVINCE OF
BRITISH COLUMBIA
19 67

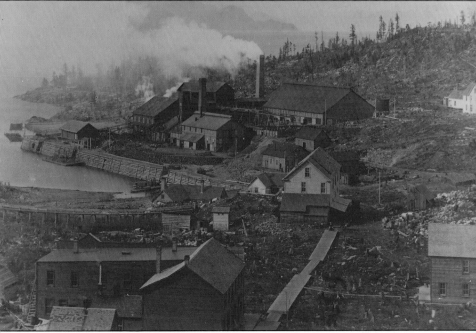

Sproule guilty of the murder of Hammill, but recommended mercy. Sproule's defence lawyer asked that the jury be polled, but his motion was denied. The judge also ignored the recommendation for mercy and sentenced Sproule to be hanged on January 5, 1886.

While Sproule was returned to jail to await execution, a furore erupted over his trial. Three of the jurors swore affidavits to the effect that they had only agreed to the guilty verdict because they had been assured that, with the recommendation for mercy, Sproule would escape the death penalty. The behaviour of Adam and Charles Wolfe became even more extraordinary. On being told that he would have to testify against Sproule, Adam was said to have butted his head against a tree in a effort to kill himself. After the conviction of Sproule, both he and Charles swore affidavits before the sheriff in Sandpoint to the effect that their evidence at the trial was, in all essential particulars, untrue, and that they were induced to give evidence by Constable Anderson because they were suspected of being parties to the murder. They also stated that they were promised $500 and expenses for giving evidence.

The other Sproule employee, Charles House, did not even testify; but after Sproule's conviction he signed a statement before H. Squire, Clerk of the First Judicial Court of Idaho Territory, stating that in October, 1885, he saw Constable Anderson in Sandpoint. Anderson, he declared, told him that Captain Ainsworth was offering a reward for evidence which would convict Sproule. He quoted Anderson as saying, "If you know anything against Sproule, tell me, and I will see that you get well paid for it." House also declared that Sproule did not borrow Adam Wolfe's gun, and the gun was not examined by anyone at lunchtime. When all these conflicting statements were given full coverage by the press, the public became aroused and angered by the law's determination to uphold the conviction of Sproule. A public meeting was held in Victoria, chaired by the mayor himself, and a full review of the case was demanded.

*(Below left) William Baillie-Grohman in his home at "Schloss Matzin."*
*(Below right) Two rival stern-wheelers, the* **International** *and the* **Moyie** *at the original Bluebell mine site near Riondel, c1905.*

Three times the dreaded day of execution hovered over Sproule, and three times it was stayed while another legal hassle was fought over his case. Finally, on October 29, 1886, Sproule was led to the gallows. He begged the hangman not to strangle him and again protested his innocence; then the trap was sprung.

The New York *Tribune* of November 4, 1886 editorialized: "The hanging of Robert Sproule at Victoria, B.C. entails a fearful responsibility on the Canadian government. Evidence of Sproule's innocence is so strong as to have convinced the public that he was wrongly convicted."

Of course, Sproule would never be found guilty today, and, even in 1885, another suspect in the murder of Hammill might have been found. Hammill's arrogant manner made him many enemies, and he regarded the Indians in the camp as inferiors and treated them with contempt. The two Wolfe brothers and possibly Charles House were part Indian, and if authorities had taken the trouble to unravel their skein of bewildering statements it might have been discovered that one of them shot Hammill. But with the hanging of Sproule the case was closed.

The Ainsworth interests took over the Bluebell. However they did not re-record the property and it reverted to the Crown. Then, in 1886, Dr. Hendryx, representing eastern capital, opened a new era in the Bluebell's, and the Kootenays', industrial history. Although Hendryx was not a prospector, he had strong backing and good business sense. He forecast a great mining empire, and he wasted no time forging plans into realities.

A tote road was built north from Sandpoint to Bonner's Ferry on the Kootenay River. There a small towboat was launched for freighting supplies to the Bluebell.

Underground development, started in 1887, saw some 1,500 feet of workings driven and half-a-million tons of ore proved within three years. By 1895 the new owners had a mill and smelter at Pilot Bay, eight miles south of the mine, and 52,000 tons of high-grade lead ore ready for treatment.

However, work stopped in 1896 "pending completion of the Crows Nest Pass branch of the Canadian Pacific Railway which would make cheaper fuel available and reduce transportation costs which prohibited the operation of mine and smelter at a profit."

Rue du Quatre-Septembre, Paris, France was an unlikely address for the head office of the Canadian Metal Company listing zinc works at Frank, Alberta, and the Bluebell mine on its letterhead. Yet it was from Paris that money came to keep the Bluebell hopes alive.

Edouard, Count Riondel, was president. Representing him in faraway British Columbia was Samuel S. Fowler, soon to become well known in Canadian mining, and British Columbia historical organizations.

From 1905 to the end of the First World War, the Canadian Metal Company advanced the fortunes of "the mine with the enchanting floral name." But as the workings went deeper, water problems multiplied. In 1921, the French directorate voted itself out of existence.

Three years later, Fowler, in partnership with B.L. Eastman, added "New" to the old company's name and tried again. The mine was de-watered, flotation equipment was added to a mill on the site, and lead and zinc concentrates were shipped to the Consolidated Mining and Smelting Company's (COMINCO) smelter at Trail.

After considering such names as Douglas, McDonald, Hammill and Hendryx, not to mention Bluebell, Fowler finally chose Riondel to identify the post office of which

*(Above left) Angus Davis at the Bluebell mine site c1910-12.*
*(Above right) The remains of the Bluebell mine's dock in May, 1985.*
*(Opposite page, top) The foundation and ruins of Cominco's Bluebell mine mill with Kootenay Lake in the background.*
*(Opposite page, bottom) The foundation of the old mill operated by Fowler at the original Bluebell mine, about a quarter of a mile from Cominco's Bluebell mine site.*

he became postmaster.

But low metal prices, the inroads of hot spring water and shortage of power doomed the enterprise. The Bluebell closed in 1927 after yielding 557,000 tons of ore.

Then COMINCO, which had financed much of the Fowler-Eastman activity, acquired ownership. Unfortunately, the Great Depression and the Second World War followed in quick succession, and the Bluebell mine rested on its raucous laurels for another 20 years.

It was not until 1947 that new ideas about its geology sparked close re-examination of the property and adjoining claims. Diamond drilling outlined significant ore at depth. Plans for a modern concentrator were drawn up, its completion synchronized with the crossing of Kootenay Lake by one of the world's largest power spans.

On April 15, 1952, the mill went into operation. It supplied the Trail smelter continuously until late 1971 when reserves of "economic" ore were exhausted.

Mining camps, like people, must retire sooner or later. Some, their workaday reason for living gone, manage to cling despondently to life for but a few years before inactivity kills them. Others seize upon retirement as an opportunity to do things they have dreamed about all their lives. They never seem to die. Riondel, one the oldest mining camps in British Columbia, retired at the end of 1971. But the final flooding of the Bluebell prompted little despondency. The future of the community as a retirement and recreation centre, although quite a change from the past, seems assured. ♣

# 2
# AINSWORTH:
# WEST KOOTENAY'S FIRST TOWN

*Named in honour of an American capitalist, the silver town on the west shore of Kootenay Lake soon attracted prospectors and mining promoters. For a time it boomed, but with the falling silver prices, Ainsworth began a steady decline. Today, a half-dozen original buildings remain at the site.*

ALTHOUGH the first quartz locations in the Kootenay Lake country were made at Galena Bay, Ainsworth was the first town in West Kootenay to come into being, appearing on maps under that name as early as 1887. But its history goes back even further. The area first drew attention when miners working on the Bluebell and Kootenay Chief mines, across Kootenay Lake, were intrigued by a band of limestone bluffs. In the summer of 1883, Thomas Hammill located five claims here for Capt. George J. Ainsworth, an American capitalist, who was a prominent mining and transportation promoter in the area.

While the 166-acre site, first known as Hot Springs Camp, was not platted into lots until 1888, it had begun to take on the shape of a town when Alfred D. Wheeler landed there in the spring of 1884. Wheeler discovered high-grade silver ore 1,000 feet above the lake. Naming the mine Krao, after his dog, he set to work using hand drills and dynamite. That summer Charles Olson and his partner located the Highland claim, destined to become the largest producer in the British Empire. As the strikes continued on the upper reaches of Princess, Cedar, Krao, Coffee and Woodbury creeks, it soon became obvious that Hot Springs Camp was destined to become a bona-fide mining town.

As word of the finds leaked out, prospectors began streaming across the border from Montana, the Cour d'Alenes and Washington state. A surprising number were old acquaintances from the placers of Granite Creek in the Tulameen.

In 1888, Gustavus B. Wright, the famous Cariboo Wagon Road contractor, acting as Captain Ainsworth's agent, laid out a town-site and plotted 45, 25x100-foot lots. Two streets, on either side of Wright's log general store, were named Wright and Sutton. By 1890, a third of the lots had been sold at prices ranging from $100 to $150, and 15 to 20 buildings had been erected.

The first establishment to open for business was Wright's general store. But Wright soon became involved with other enterprises and sold out to Fletcher & Company. On July 26, 1890, they placed Ainsworth's first business ad in the first issue of the Nelson *Miner,* offering miner's supplies, provisions, tools, crockery, clothing and stationery for sale.

The owner of the first hotel is not as easy to determine, but by mid-June, 1890, two were under construction; Laatz & McLeod's Sproatle Hotel and A.A. McKinnon's Vancouver House. Another pioneer businessman was Henry Anderson, who, in addition to being a constable, was a real estate agent and notary public. Ainsworth residents, being a mixture of Americans and Canadians, celebrated both July 1 and July 4. According to the Nelson *Miner,* July 1 was celebrated "...by exploding a great amount of giant powder and consuming the average amount of fire water. On the 4th the principal events were boat races, in which many of the best-known oarsmen of the camp took an active part — seated around hotel stoves."

Meanwhile, mining operations above the town were not amounting to much more than assessment work and prospecting. Granted, small quantities of ore had previously been shipped to American smelters, but only with great difficulty and expense. The problem was transportation, for, while the steamers *Galena* and *Idaho* could easily move the ore to market from the lake shore, getting the ore there from the mines was much more difficult.

To overcome this problem, Wheeler began construction of a wagon road from the town to the mines on July 9, 1890. Despite a shortage of manpower, work progressed so rapidly that within two weeks most of the right-of-way had been cleared and the first half-mile was graded. By the end of August, the road had been completed to the Krao.

As new mines were discovered and existing mines began shipping ore, Ainsworth's future seemed assured. E.S. Wilson & Company, owners of a general store in Revelstoke, were so convinced of the town's future prospects that they purchased a lot on Wright Street in July and began erecting a two-story, 22x55-foot store. On July 21, amidst all the early construction and activity, Mrs. George Harmon gave birth to a 13-pound baby girl, the first white child to be born anywhere in Kootenay Lake country.

On August 30, in what the Nelson *Miner* proclaimed as "The social event of the season," W.J. McKinney's hotel opened for business. "The hotel building is new and 25x62 feet in size, and will be elegantly furnished throughout." At the same time carpenters were busy constructing John McNeill's Columbia Hotel, and A.E. Bryan, formerly with the Anaconda Company of Butte, Montana, was establishing an assay office. Ainsworth now had an estimated 200 residents in the town and nearby hills, but it lamented the fact that it still lacked a post office.

As more mines entered production, it seemed only natural to establish a smelter in the area. Thus, in September, a man named Best selected a suitable site at the mouth of Woodbury Creek, two miles north of Ainsworth. The smelter, with a 20-ton capacity, was scheduled for a trial run on October 17 after a test made earlier that week had proved satisfactory. But the trial run had to be delayed when the owners of the pack train refused to transport the ore from the mines for the price offered. Alas, it was a short reprieve for the smelter, for, during the first day of its trial run the heat generated proved to be too great.

"The Best smelter split in two making its first trial run," reported the *Miner.* "Those present state that it was because of the faulty construction of the plant, its foundation being laid on ground intermixed with decayed tree roots." As he left Ainsworth, Best promised to return in the fall to erect another smelter at or near the Krao, but it was not to be.

In mid-September the town-site owners, through agent W.W. Sprague, Wright having resigned, announced that the town would be surveyed in the fall. The

(Above) Capt. George J. Ainsworth, after whom the town of Ainsworth was named.
(Opposite page) The Silver Ledge Hotel, on Ainsworth's main street, is now a museum.
(Left) The front of the Silver Ledge Hotel.
(Below) The main street of Ainsworth as it appeared in the early 1890s.

following month, McKinnon's Vancouver House, the "largest and best situated hotel in Ainsworth," had been completed, Wright's warehouse at the wharf was nearly finished, and Joseph Fletcher and his partner had dug the foundation for a new business establishment which they expected to build shortly.

In November the owners of the United mine extended the government wagon road from the Krao to the United, a distance of about half a mile. During the same month it was reported that George Ainsworth had sold the town-site to a syndicate of Montreal capitalists associated with G.B. Wright. There were now between 200 and 300 claims in the area, although not more than 15 mines were presently being worked.

By this time Ainsworth was starting to get competition from the upstart community of Balfour. Determined not ". . . to let Balfour get away with the baggage of Hot Springs Camp," the town-site owners proposed to erect a crib wharf that would extend 400 feet into the lake. "It will be so built that landings can be made on either side, and will be large enough to accommodate the steamers of both the Hendryx and Mara lines."

As winter descended upon the district, mining activity slowed considerable and the town's population dwindling to about 150. The town itself, however, remained relatively buoyant, with an estimated $10,000 being expended on new buildings and improvements. The town now boasted two merchandise stores, four hotels and saloons, and a number of residences. Another positive note occurred on December 9, when Ainsworth finally got its own post office.

All was not rosy, however. One of the merchants, E.S. Wilson, who had regularly placed quarter-page ads in the *Miner*, was in financial difficulty. Unfortunately, although Wilson's Ainsworth store was apparently doing a flourishing business, the main store at Revelstoke was losing money. Creditors were closing in, and in January, 1891, Mr. Cornell of the Winnipeg firm of Cornell, Spera & Company, was appointed as the assignee. In March both stores, with liabilities of about $20,000, were closed, although it was hoped the Ainsworth store might reopen. Unfortunately, it was not to be and in May, the entire stock was sold to Robert and Samuel Green. The Green Brothers operated stores at Illecillewaet and Sproat and had been contemplating opening a store at Ainsworth for some time. As for Wilson, he rebounded from his loss and was appointed a notary public.

The result of the winter's work in mine development gave the businessmen of Ainsworth renewed confidence in the permanency of their town. As a result, substantial additions were completed in the spring of 1891. McKinnon erected a two-story, 24x60-foot addition to the Vancouver House; Fletcher & McKay graded the ground for a 24x36-foot, two-story addition to their business; Roderick McLeod was completing a large 25x100-foot addition to his Palace Hotel, and McNeill & Bromberg were putting the finishing touches to the inside of their hotel.

Among the new establishments were Wilson & Perdue's 20x30-foot meat market; J.L. Retallack's livery barn and food stable and Olson & Williamson's two-story, 30x60-foot hotel. Other businesses included a drug store, operated by Dr. Henry of Spokane; a general store, operated by the Spokane Mercantile Company; a notions and fancy goods store, owned by Mrs. Adams and Mrs. Schroeder's restaurant. Elsewhere, J.G. McGuigan and J. Martin had the frame of their two-story building up. When completed, the building would be occupied by J.H. Fink for general merchandise. At the end of May, Dad's Chap House, "the only short order house in Hot Springs district," opened its doors. Specializing in porterhouse and tenderloin steaks, proprietor Josiah Brown promised meals at all hours. In June, Bremner & Watson established a pack and saddle horse business and Alfred Stalberg opened the Germania Assay Office.

In July, the Lindsay Mercantile Company sold its stock of goods to Henry Giegerich, who had arrived in town from Anaconda. The following month Giegerich also acquired Fletcher's store and merchandise. Fletcher also sold his interest in the Club Saloon to Tom Devlin, and he was now free to pursue his mining interests.

In early September, telephone communication was established between Ainsworth and Buchanan's sawmill, and by mid-month connection was made with Nelson. The telegraph also connected Ainsworth with the outside world.

On September 12, Ainsworth took another step towards respectability when the first issue of its own weekly newspaper, the *Hot Springs News* made its appearance. The paper was published each Saturday by John Houston and Charles Ink of Nelson. They were also publishers of the Nelson *Miner,* the first newspaper to be published in West Kootenay.

In the first issue of the *Hot Springs News,* the residents of Ainsworth complained that the town-site owners, having acquired the only water rights for supplying the town with water for household and fire purposes, would "neither utilize it nor allow other people to utilize it. Owing to the topography of the townsite," they argued, "the buildings are pretty closely huddled, and should a fire break out, it would be almost impossible to save the town from destruction."

The first issue also carried ads for a number of Ainsworth businesses. Bremner & Watson offered pack and saddle horses for hire. They also acted as agents for the Davis-Sayward Sawmill, offering lumber, moulding and shingles. A.E. Bryan advertised his services as assayer and chemist, while J.A. Melville was an architect, contractor and builder. In large quarter-page ads, Green Brothers offered miners' supplies, iron and steel, hardware, groceries, boots and shoes, dry goods, clothing and men's furnishings. Robert Green was also the postmaster. Henry Anderson and John Retallack, having joined forces, were conducting a general real estate office, mine brokerage and conveyancing business under the name of Anderson & Retallack.

Although church services had been held in an Ainsworth hotel as early as August, 1890, and had been well attended, the town was still without its own church. That soon changed, however, as in its second issue, the *News* reported that "Rev. Mr. Turner, of the Methodist persuasion is erecting a church at Ainsworth. The building is on a lot fronting the wagon road to the Krao and other mines."

In October, the telephone company put in a switchboard and established a central office in Green Brothers general store. This led to an amusing incident when Jack Hennessey, an employee of the Number One mine, tried to place a call. Hennessey had never seen or used a telephone until he saw one at the mine. The *News* picks up the story. "One day, upon putting the receiver to his ear for the first time, the crackling noise made by a defective battery in the central office at Green's store, alarmed him, and he rushed from the room shouting, 'Boys! Boys! Green's store is afire!' He started down the mountainside on a dead run, and was at the store, four miles distant, in 25 minutes, only to find that establishment standing as when he last saw it." Hennessey would survive this embarrassment and go on to locate, with four others, the famous Noble Five mine at Sandon.

(Opposite page, top left) The kitchen of the historic Silver Ledge Hotel showing a McClary's stove.
(Opposite page, top right) A bedroom in the Silver Ledge Hotel.

(Left) An old writing desk inside the Silver Ledge Hotel. The Hotel is now a museum and is open to visitors during the summer months. These three photos were taken in August, 1989.

(Below) A view of Ainsworth from the waterfront in 1898. By this time Ainsworth was overshadowed by the rich mines of the Slocan.

Ainsworth experienced its greatest growth in 1891, and it appeared like there was no limit to what the town would achieve. It was the oldest of the three established town in West Kootenay, Ainsworth, Sproat and Nelson, and ranked second in size behind Nelson. Its future seemed bright. But in late September, Eli Carpenter and Jack Seaton made rich new discoveries in the Slocan that did not bode well for the small mining camp. Virtually overnight an exodus began, and on October 3 the *Miner* reported: "The Kaslo-Slocan excitement has almost depopulated Ainsworth, but one woman (Mrs. Trenery) being left in the town. All the others, men and women, have gone to Kaslo City, 12 miles up the lake from Ainsworth and the place at which prospectors debark for the new district on the divide between Kaslo creek and Slocan lake. However, they are all likely to return and winter at Ainsworth."

In the first heady days of the rush many of Ainsworth's merchants did a thriving business by outfitting hopeful prospectors. After that, however, the town settled in for the winter, uncertain what the future held. As expected, many residents did return, and, with all the mining activity in the nearby mountains, there was never any real danger of Ainsworth dying completely. But these new discoveries would shift the centre of attention from Ainsworth to the new town of Kaslo, and later, to Sandon, at the very heart of the silver mines.

However Ainsworth businessmen were sufficiently concerned that, on December 23, they held a public meeting to discuss the situation and determine a course of action. Many felt that if Ainsworth was to remain "in the race," the streets would have to be graded and public improvements made. But there was no money for improvements and the town-site owners seemed unwilling to help.

"One of the improvements most needed is a wharf," reported the *News,* "but, judging from the opinions expressed at the meeting, there seems to be a doubt as to where is should be built, one faction claiming that the present wharf is at the best site, and the other that it should be built further to the south."

Four men, Jevons, Watson, Bremner and Lovatt, came to the conclusion that, in order to survive and prosper, Ainsworth had to be headquarters for other interests beside mining. To this end, in January, 1892, they began construction of an 80-foot stern-wheeler with powerful machinery. Reporting on the launching, which occurred on May 3, the *News* wrote: "Owing to a rope breaking, the stern started down the ways before the bow, tearing away the guide-ways. The result was the boat struck the water first on her starboard quarter and the bow left the ways and took the ground about 10 feet from the stern. The *Galena,* however, after one or two attempts, was successful in towing her off without damage."

Alas, this was only the beginning of the *Ainsworth's* problems. The hull was towed to Bonner's Ferry, where the engine and boiler were to be installed. But on June 8 the *News* reported: "The steamer *Ainsworth* is tied up at the customs station at Rykert. The owners are unable to get her away as it is asserted that before she can be released it will be necessary for her to be examined, not only by the boiler inspector, but by an inspecting board; and this because the boiler was made in Chicago, and has some patent fuel-saving apparatus attached."

This angered the *News,* and in an editorial in the same issue they demanded to know why the "*Ainsworth* is tied up in idleness, waiting for an inspection that never comes. Is it because she has on board an American improvement on Canadian made machinery, or is it because she is opposed to interests of a corporation whose interests are paramount in this country."

Typical of early frontier newspapers, where problems and solutions were sometimes printed in the same issue, another column reported: "The camp turned out in force on Tuesday night to welcome the return of the steamer *Ainsworth*. She was greeted with a salute of dynamite and three hearty cheers."

Ironically, the steamer that had been built to promote the town it was named after, did not base itself at Ainsworth for very long. Instead, as Kaslo grew in importance, the new owners used that town as its main centre of operations.

Meanwhile, in the spring of 1892, Ainsworth town lots, apparently not yet negatively affected by Kaslo and the Slocan, were being offered for $1,000. At the waterfront, aided by a $1,500 government contribution, construction of a new wharf was well underway. In the town itself, the main problem concerning businessmen was drainage. Unfortunately, the town was divided over the issue. Some property owners were willing to pay their share of the expense, others were not, while still others were simply indifferent to the entire matter. Commenting on the situation, the *News* wrote: "The townsite is owned by a company that appears to oppose every improvement that the residents of the place favor, and the result is that the town is without a water system, without graded streets, without drainage and without many more conveniences that are actually necessary. Unless something is done in a way of drainage epidemic disease will be the result, and the loss of a few lives will probably cause those most directly interested to bestir themselves."

But Ainsworth's days of glory were over. As Kaslo and Sandon increased in importance, Ainsworth declined. In March, assayer Bryan moved his office to Kaslo. In May, the following ad appeared in the *News:* "A half interest in the bar of the Ainsworth house at Ainsworth and the whole of the furniture, etc., of that hotel is for sale, including 50 cords of wood, 15 tons of ice, and 100 chickens. The hotel has 16 bedrooms and is doing a business of $75 a day, the bar is doing a business of $30 a day. Price $2,100 cash." During the same month the *News* was sold to Boyle & Whalley, the original owners apparently seeing the writing on the wall. In July, Ainsworth suffered a major setback when its wharf was destroyed. "The new wharf has succumbed to the united attacks of steamboats and waves," reported the *News.* "Owing to the nature of the bed of the lake the piles lifted and the wharf does not now exist."

As the months of 1892 dragged by, other signs of the town's ill health became apparent; business fell off and partnerships were dissolved. The first came on August 20 when the owners of the *Ainsworth* dissolved their partnership. Five days later R. Reiuonald and W.A. Skinner dissolved their contracting and building business. On September 5, Anderson & Retallack dissolved their partnership, Anderson continuing on alone. The following month, with little news to report and fewer advertisers to support it, the newspaper itself folded.

Ainsworth was in a steady decline, but it would not die. Its mines continued to produce and new claims were continually being discovered. Thus the little town on the lake struggled on for the next four years. Then, on Sunday, April 26, 1896, the greatest threat faced by wooden frontier towns was realized. It was about 11:30 at night when a fire started in the Columbia Hotel. It quickly spread to the Windsor Hotel, and from there to Captain Preston's two buildings. The next to go was the Ainsworth Hotel and A. Stalberg's residence. From there, aided by the wind, the fire crossed the street to the Vancouver House, the Club Saloon, a building occupied

*(Above) This family photograph, which was taken in Ainsworth in 1891, shows Henry and Mrs. Giegerich, Henry's mother and Mrs. Hendryx.*
*(Opposite page, top) Ore shipment at the Ainsworth wharf in 1897. Mr. E.R. Nipond driving one of his six-horse freighting teams.*
*(Opposite page, bottom) A general view of Ainsworth after the fire of 1896.*
*(Below) Two views of the J.B. Fletcher store, Ainsworth. It was built in 1896 to replace the original log store destroyed in the fire. When the photo on the left was taken in 1985, the building was being restored with a $50,000 Heritage Trust grant. The photo on the right, taken in 1989, shows the completed store. It is now a museum.*

by the Ainsworth Trading Company and Ernest Harrop's building. The last to go was Giegerich's general store. Green Brothers' emporium was on fire in half a dozen places, but was saved by fire fighters.

Despite the destruction caused by the fire, however, it would have been even worst if not for the prompt actions of the fire brigade, led by T.J. Lendrum, and the actions of concerned citizens. The ladies earned particular praise for "the coolness and energy they displayed in saving goods from the buildings, some of them carrying out bundles and trunks they would not have been able to move at any other time."

The hardest hit was A.A. McKinnon, whose Vancouver House was not insured and he had been unable to save much of the furniture. Despite this, McKinnon vowed to rebuild as quickly as possible, as did many of the other businesses. It was a serious setback, but Ainsworth rose quickly from the ashes. In a little over a month McKinnon and Olson had each built new hotels, and Giegerich was erecting his new store. By September, the Ainsworth Trading Company had moved into their new premises.

Ainsworth survived the fire just as it had survived the depression caused by slumping silver prices in 1893. But the discovery of larger and richer deposits in the Silvery Slocan slowed development and ensured that Ainsworth would never attain greatness.

There was increased mining actively in 1897, but falling silver prices proved disastrous and many of the properties lay idle. The Number One mine, under L. Shaw, maintained an output of high grade concentrates, while the Skyline and Neosha were shut down. The Highland property installed an aerial tramway and concentrator, but little or no ore was taken out during the year. The Canadian Pacific Milling Company, at the mouth of Woodbury Creek, after installing a fine concentrator, was shortly afterwards forced to shut down for lack of ore.

While Ainsworth was gradually slipping, slowly becoming a secondary camp, to the west, the Slocan was humming with activity and earning its title "The Silvery Slocan." As the years passed there were times, increasingly rare, when hopes for the future of the town ran high, days when magnificent ore bodies were discovered.

During the spring of 1923, the news that the Florence mine had been acquired under option by Detroit capitalists created a stir, and big developments were expected. Unfortunately, things did not materialize and the deal fell through before any marked progress had been made. After the rights under the option on the Florence had been relinquished, R.W. Lloyd, the superintendent, and three or four others took a lease on the mine and mill. The company had a few men working under contract to advance the No. 2 level. Using a Mancha storage battery locomotive for underground and surface haulage, their work was watched with interest, for it was hoped it would lead to the development of a rich ore-body.

But the respites were few and far between, and by the end of 1925, although the Florence Silver Mining Company had been reorganized and incorporated as the Florence Consolidated Mining Company, no work was performed during the season. During the same year the Highland mine, employing 16, was worked by the Consolidated Mining & Smelting Company. Meanwhile, the Albion, Silver Hoard, Number One, Spokane-Trinket and Tariff were worked in a small way by leases.

Mining activity in the vicinity of Ainsworth during 1926 was confined to minor operations of leases at a number of properties. The average price of silver during

(Top) *A group of men at the foot of Ainsworth's main street in 1894.*
(Below) *Miners pose for a photograph at William Braden's Tariff mine, located one mile south of Ainsworth.*

*(Right) This original coffee grinder was brought up from Bonner's Ferry. It is on display in the restored J.B. Fletcher store museum in Ainsworth.*

*(Opposite page) This old scale and cash register can be seen in the J.B. Fletcher store.*

*(Below) The restored J.B. Fletcher store museum has many interesting items on display, such as food and drug items. One of the more fascinating displays is this original cheese cutter. All three photos were taken in 1989.*

the year was 62¢, as compared with 69¢ in 1925 and $1.10 in 1890. More frightening, however, was its plunge to 54¢ an ounce for the last three months of 1926. By the 1930s, when the price of silver had touched a new low, even the most optimistic of the camp's backers were hard pressed to find reasons for their faith.

By the time the depression came to a close the flagging fortunes of Ainsworth had decided its fate. Never again would the heady buoyancy of the 1890s be repeated. The few sporadic flurries thereafter were generally just that, flurries, and nothing more.

Today Ainsworth is a resort town founded on the world-wide appeal of its hot springs and the Cody Caves, a deep labyrinth of underground caverns. However, a couple of buildings from its historic past still survive. The Silver Ledge Hotel still overlooks the main street as it did more than three-quarters of a century ago when it was the Grant King Hotel. It is now a museum open to the public during the summer season.

Farther down the street, J.B. Fletcher's old general store, silent for so long, is also a museum. Through joint financing by Heritage Trust and a grant from the provincial Job Trac program, the building has been totally restored.

When the original log store was constructed by Gustavus Wright in the late 1880s, it was the first store in Ainsworth. As late as 1890, with no hotels yet built in the town, visitors sometimes slept on the floor in the store. That same year Wright sold the store to Lindsay & Fletcher Mercantile, who in turn resold it later that year to Henry Giegerich of Montana. Giegerich eventually went on to establish additional stores in Kaslo, Three Forks and Sandon.

When the original log store was destroyed in the fire of 1896, Giegerich constructed the present building, which was managed for some time by J.H. Fink. In 1912, John Bradley Fletcher came in from Cranbrook to replace Fink. Fletcher managed the store until the 1920s when he purchased it, changing the name to the way it appears today. Fletcher and his wife operated the store for 60 years before his death in 1974. Both he and his wife are buried in the Ainsworth cemetery. ♣

# 3
# HISTORIC NELSON &
# THE FABLED SILVER KING

*When their search for placer gold along the Salmon River proved
fruitless, the prospectors made plans to leave. While rounding up
the horses on a nearby mountain, they accidentally discovered a rich
silver outcrop. Their find attracted a number of other miners and led to
the establishment of Nelson, the oldest city in West Kootenay.*

IT was late in August, 1886, when a party of prospectors from Fort Colville, now
Colville, Washington, loaded provisions into boats and rowed up the Columbia
River. The 14-man party, led by the brothers Osner and Winslow Hall, included
their six sons, two cousins named Oakes, two close friends, Willis White and Will
Miller, and two Indian boys. It turned out later that the Indian boys was not consi-
dered to have the same status as the others.

The expedition had been born out of desperation and hope. For several years,
farmers from Colville had been selling their produce to the construction gangs
building the Canadian Pacific Railway (CPR) mainline through British Columbia
from Revelstoke. But now the construction was finished and, to make matters
worst, it was a year of crop failures.

In the face of all this, it was perfectly natural for the Hall brothers to organize
a party to search for placer gold. Crossing the border into British Columbia, they
followed the Pend D'Oreille River to Beaver Creek, which was followed to the
Salmon River. From there they worked their way up what is now the Hall Creek
basin behind Toad Mountain. It meant about 100 miles of sweaty, exhausting labour,
cutting a trail out of the forest the entire distance for their 21 pack horses. Along
the way they stopped to pan the creeks, but never did they find more than a trace
of gold.

Throughout the entire region of West Kootenay in 1886 there was not a single
town. Hot Springs Camp, a small settlement about 30 miles north of their present
position, was the only sign of "civilization." But even it would not begin to take
the shape of a town for another year. The district had no roads or railroads; boats
and crude trails being the only means of transportation. Alone in this vast isolation,
it is not difficult to understand how the prospectors became disillusioned by their
lack of success. To make matters worst, it was now October and there was a strong
indication of any early winter in the air. All things considered, Winslow Hall, the
party's leader, decided they would prospect one more day. If nothing was found,
they would abandon their quest and return to Colville.

The party had made their camp on a tributary of the Salmon River, now known
as Hall Creek, which wound its way down an as yet unnamed mountain where they

found good feed for the horse. As the main party broke camp for a final day of gold prospecting, Winslow instructed his son Tommy, and Billy White, to round up the horses in preparation for the next day's departure.

While the boys were thus engaged, they stumbled across the outcrop of what later became the Kootenay Bonanza. The boys had no knowledge of exactly what they had discovered, but, believing the mineralized rock to be gold, picked up several pieces each. On the way back to camp they startled some grouse, and Tommy Hall used up his samples by throwing them at the birds. White had kept his specimens, however, and upon showing them to the others in camp, they decided to return to the outcrop the following day.

The next day the party returned to the location of the outcrop and secured several more specimens, which were then taken to Colville. There, some of the samples were given to Colonel Linsley, an assayer, for analysis. Linsley reported that the ore was worthless, but he appeared very anxious to learn where they came from. However, except to state that it was near navigable water, Winslow refused to divulge the source. Meanwhile, another Colville assayer, Jake Cobaugh, reported that the samples were rich in silver. Winslow was so pleased by this report that he gave Cobaugh a one-thirteenth interest in the mine.

The Hall party spent an anxious winter in Colville. The apparent richness of their mine created a great deal of excitement among the discoverers. But their ecstasy was dampened by the fact that they had not staked any claims. Now they could not risk word of their discovery leaking out before they had it all sewn up legally and correctly.

In a place the size of Colville, however, it was difficult to keep things quiet. Certainly the news reached a Scot, John Macdonald, who offered himself as their manager and was immediately accepted. Macdonald then decreed that the two Indian boys, Narcisse Downing and Dawney Williams, had only been hired hunters in the original expedition. He paid them $250 each and told them they were no longer required. Downing and Williams both had Canadian miners' licenses and both had been present when the great strike on Toad Mountain was made. It is easy to understand their resentment at being pushed out of the picture.

When the Halls left on their second expedition to West Kootenay in the spring of 1887, it seems that half the town of Colville followed after them. The Hall party started for the site of their discovery by the Salmon River route. The snow was too deep, however, so they went back and came in by way of Bonner's Ferry. Travelling down Kootenay Lake by boat, they landed at what was shortly to be the town-site of Nelson, and reached their goal well ahead of the stampeders. On July 9, 1887, Thomas Hall, William White and William Oakes located the Kootenay Bonanza on the divide between Cottonwood Smith and Salmon creeks. Later that day other members of the party located the Silver King and American Flag. They gave their venture the official name Kootenay Bonanza Company. But where did they register their claims?

According to a history of the area that appeared in the March 23, 1893 issue of the Nelson *Tribune*, "Della" Fry acted as mining recorder in the district during the fall and winter of 1887-88 and up to the appointment of Henry Anderson. This statement was made by James Fox, who landed on the mountain shortly after the Hall party. Fox was present when the first stake was planted on the Kootenay Bonanza. He further went on to state that Fry would not record assessment work

**(Above)** *A log cabin at the Silver King mine.*
**(Right)** *Gold Commissioner Gilbert Malcolm Sproat. After visiting Nelson in 1888, he was instructed to lay-out a town-site.*
**(Below)** *The Silver King mine site, on Toad Mountain, in the early 1890s. Its discovery set the foundation upon which the city of Nelson sprang into existence.*

because he felt he lacked the power to do so. "Claim owners, therefore, had to make the records at Fort Steele or Revelstoke, several of the assessments being recorded at both places."

However, Gilbert Malcolm Sproat, who was in charge of the entire district from Farwell (Revelstoke), and later became the region's gold commissioner, claimed otherwise. In a letter which appeared in the Nelson *Miner* on October 9, 1897, he wrote: ". . . no Kootenay Lake or Toad Mountain records were taken, or could be legally made, at Farwell until after March 14, 1888. If received there they were passed on to Mr. Vowell at Donald." However, this is further complicated by a story that appeared in Sandon's *Slocan Mining Recorder* on June 6, 1907. In the article, Alfred Wheeler claims that, although he was an American citizen, he had been appointed mining recorder by the provincial government when the rush on Toad Mountain started. He says he recorded the Hall claims but he does not state where. (Wheeler, you may recall, landed in Ainsworth in 1884.) Thus, where, when and how the claims on Toad Mountain were actually recorded remains an unsubstantiated mystery.

Meanwhile, the other prospectors who had followed the Hall party from Colville began to arrive and soon the still unnamed mountain began to look like an anthill. On July 27, Ben Thomas and Charlie Townsend located a claim called the Jim Crow on the west side of Giveout Creek. While Thomas was cutting stakes for this claim, Townsend was sitting on a log about a foot off the ground writing the claim notice. When he had completed the notice as far as "situate on," a big toad suddenly jumped from under the log and landed near his feet. Thus, Townsend named the place "Toad" Mountain. This is the first time in which any name had been designated for the mountain.

On October 15, Thomas "Sandy" Morrow recorded the Toughnut claim and described it as being "situate about four miles west of the Bonanza camp, Mineral mountain, in Kootenai (sic) mining district, B.C." This was the first claim in which the name "Mineral" Mountain was used. On March 1, 1888, N. Hoover and James McKenzie located the Porcupine claim, two and a-half miles west of the Silver King on "Mineral" Mountain. A number of other locations were also recorded in March of that year, and all were described on "Mineral" Mountain. On May 7, P.J. McDougal recorded the Poorman, once again giving the location as Mineral Mountain. All the claims mentioned above as being recorded in 1887, plus others not mentioned, were either relocated or rerecorded in 1888, and all were described as being on Mineral Mountain — even the Jim Crow, which had originally been stated as Toad Mountain. How then, did Toad Mountain become the designated name?

In April or May of 1888, Henry Anderson, newly-appointed mining recorded for the district, arrived on the scene from Ainsworth. Anderson apparently favoured the name Mineral Mountain. Anderson also gave the name "Salisbury" to the embryo town starting to take shape on the lake shore. When Gold Commissioner Sproat arrived later that year, however, things began to change. There was apparently no love lost between Sproat and Anderson. Although Sproat denied he harboured ill feelings toward Anderson in a letter he wrote to the Nelson *Tribune* in 1893, Thomas Collins, a pioneer in the region as early as 1880, made it clear that Anderson, at least, had no use for Sproat. He even went further by claiming that Sproat was disliked by many old-timers in the region.

In any event, Sproat favoured the name Toad Mountain. Similarly, he renamed the town "Stanley." Both men were bull-headed, and for a time, the town was officially designated "Salisbury" by the mining recorder, and "Stanley" by the gold commissioner. The feud continued until Sproat resigned in 1888-89, being replaced by G.C. Tunstall. The town continued to be known by two names until it applied for a post office. On the application the name Stanley was used. However, since there was already a town with that name in the Cariboo, the name was changed to Nelson, in honour of Hugh Nelson, then lieutenant-governor of the province.

Prior to all the political in-fighting, back in the fall of 1887, Toad Mountain had attracted a great deal of attention. The names of those who recorded claims that year included Thomas Hall, William White, William Oakes, Winslow Hall, Osner Hall, Charles Hall, William Miller, Oscar Hall, John Hall, Richard A. Fry, Arthur C. Fry, Osner M. Oakes, James Fox, Michael Keeley, John R. Cook, Charles Townsend, Benjamin Thomas, Price McDonald, S.H. Cross, C.H. Randall, Isaac Lougheed, William Hanson, C.H. Montgomery, Charles Malle, Thomas Morrow, J.J. Hanley and John Cobb. Most of these individuals had followed the Halls from Colville.

The first area to become populated as a result of all the mining activity that followed was the upper reaches of Toad Mountain. Within a few months after the Halls staked their claims, 25 or more log cabins had been built by prospectors high

*(Right) A.S. Farwell. In the summer of 1889, he properly surveyed the original 88 Nelson lots, plus 44 more. (Below) This early view of Nelson was taken c1890. (Inset) The Lake View Hotel, one of Nelson's earliest hotels, once stood on the site of the Nelson City Hall.*

LAKE VIEW HOTEL.
NELSON, B.C. 1890

on the mountain, close to the action. Named Fredericton, this small town boasted office buildings, a sawmill, a school, and a hotel called the Grand View.

In addition, by the winter of 1887-88, 300-400 people, living mostly in tents, were scattered along Ward Creek, in what is now the centre of Nelson. The majority of these individuals were made up from the population of Donald and Revelstoke, who rushed to the area when news of the strike leaked out. When they first arrived, Arthur Bunting's solitary log cabin stood on the future town-site of Nelson. (This building stood until August, 1897, when it was demolished to make room for a new railway line connecting two railway stations.) A son-in-law of Richard Fry, the patriarch pioneer of Kootenay Lake, Bunting had taken up 160 acres and was offering lots to squatters for a nominal fee.

This was the scene that greeted Sproat during his first visit there in 1888. When he reported this to the government, however, it declared that Bunting had no title to his claim, and instructed Sproat to lay-out a town-site. With the aid of a piece of rope, Sproat laid off a portion of what is now Vernon Street, and in October, 1888, the sale of the first 88 lots took place. In the summer of 1889 these lots, together with 44 more, were properly surveyed by A.S. Farwell, and up to 1890 these 132 lots constituted the entire platted part of the Nelson town-site. Lumber was first obtainable in August, 1889, but building operations did not begin until late in the fall.

One of the first merchants of Nelson was R.E. Lemon, of Revelstoke, who first visited the area in May, 1888. Lemon left Revelstoke on May 14 with a big stock of groceries. Accompanying him on the boat were George O. Buchanan, Thomas M.

Ward, Bob Hall, Thomas Downs and Harry Sheran. (Buchanan had operated a sawmill at Illecillewaet. After looking Nelson over, he applied for a timber grant, which was awarded in December, 1888. Ward established one of Nelson's first hotels.) Lemon and the others landed at Sproat's Landing, where Lemon promptly established a store. In September, 1888, Lemon constructed a log building for a grocery store at Nelson. During construction of the Columbia & Kootenay Railway (C&K), Lemon operated stores at both locations. But in the spring following the completion of the C&K, he closed the store at Sproat's and concentrated his business at Nelson.

On Toad Mountain, meanwhile, the Halls had performed the necessary assessment work for 1888 and 1889. Then Richard Day Atkins, a native of Ireland, and his partner Mr. Ramsey, a Montana cattle rancher, offered to purchase the properties for a nominal sum. The Halls refused, demanding $1,000,000 for their claims. M.S. Davys then offered $350,000, but this was also rejected, despite the fact the Halls had no working capital.

Atkins made several more attempts to purchase the property, but when these also failed, he decided to try another approach. He offered the Halls a $20,000 loan for development of the mine, secured by a mortgage on the properties. Unfortunately, the Halls made personal use of the funds and did very little actual development work. Atkins then advanced more money, and in a comparatively short time the Halls were hopelessly in debt, while their mine remained undeveloped.

What happened next is a mystery that has never been completely resolved. It is known that three men from Victoria jumped the property on the allegation that the locations had not been made according to the Mineral Act. One must assume that this litigation centred on the mystery surrounding the original staking of the claims two years earlier. Another mystery concerns the true involvement of Atkins in the lawsuit. Some historians claim that he offered to fight the case in court for the Halls in return for a 50 percent interest. The Nelson *Miner*, however, suggests Atkins' involvement may have been far more sinister. Writing a brief history of the mine in 1897, the paper claimed that Atkins had actually hired the three claim jumpers from Victoria. He then "explained to and finally convinced the Halls that the law suit by which they were threatened would ruin them if commenced, and succeeded in obtaining one-half interest in the group in consideration for the money loaned and for stopping all legal proceedings." The Halls were probably unaware of Atkins' behind-the-scenes involvement, for there was no mention of it in the newspaper at the time. Atkins treachery, if true, did not surface until the above article appeared nearly a decade later.

Atkins, however, did not profit from his half ownership of the Silver King, regardless of how it was obtained. On August 17, 1890, following an illness of two weeks, the 49-year-old Atkins died of pneumonia in the Nelson House. He was buried in Victoria.

By this time the Silver King had $60,000 worth of first-class ore waiting on the dumps. Without a wagon road, however, transporting this ore to the waterfront remained the mine owners' most pressing problem. In the summer of 1888, Richard Fry had established a trail of sorts from the waterfront to the summit, and on this he used a train of pack mules and horses.

Fry's association with West Kootenay began in the 1860s. When the placer excitement on Wild Horse Creek was at its peak, a man named Bonner made a fortune with a trading post at what became known as Bonner's Ferry. When the rush subsided, Bonner sold out to Fry, who carried on the business of packing supplies to the miners in East Kootenay and trading with the Indians along Kootenay Lake. Fry packed his supplies in from Hope, on the Fraser River, to East Kootenay, via Bonner's Ferry, and packed his furs out by the same route. Fry spent two winters in the south Kootenay region trapping and placer mining in the 1860s. The placer grounds of 49 Mile Creek, near Nelson, received attention from Fry, and Fry Creek, on the east side of Kootenay Lake above Kaslo, is named after him. Fry even prospected in the Lardeau country.

In the spring of 1888, Fry purchased a steamer called the *Idaho,* then rusting away on Pend D'Oreille Lake. Surmounting incredible difficulties, Fry had the steamer hauled 40 miles overland to Kootenay Lake. In September, 1888, 22½ tons of ore from the Silver King was loaded onto the *Idaho* at the Nelson water-front. From there it was transported down the lake and river to Sandpoint, Idaho, and finally by rail to the smelter at Anaconda, Montana. The shipment netted $7,000. The ore carried $308 in silver and $2.50 in gold to the ton, besides being 28 percent copper.

By May, 1889, James A. Gilker was operating Nelson's first post office from a tent. Prior to this time, Eugene S. Topping, soon to be the owner of the town-site of Trail, was acting postmaster. During 1888-89, all the stamps sold in Nelson were American. Even after the post office was estab-lished, fully one-third of all the stamps sold here were United States issue.

By 1890, Nelson boasted 40-odd buildings along the waterfront, including a substantial log building that was the seat of government for lower Kootenay. Other Nelson businesses included three completed hotels, Soder-berg & Johnson's Kootenay House, Mark & Van Ness's Nelson House and Johnson & Maloney's Lakeview House. Two others, William Hunter's Inter-national and a hotel owned by Ward & Crossing, were under construction. The town also boasted three general merchants, three stables (one operated by Topping,) three notary publics, three pack trains, three real estate and mining brokers, two contractors, two clothing stores, a laundry, meat mar-ket, restaurant, post office, blacksmith and shoemaker. Of these, only the Kootenay House, Nelson House and shoemaker were identified by signs.

On June 21, 1890, the Nelson *Miner,* a weekly newspaper published by John Houston, Charles Ink and W. Gesner Allan, was started with seven subscribers. It was the first, and for a time, the only newspaper published in West Kootenay. Houston, publisher of the Donald *Truth* in 1888, followed the example of other entrepreneurs who swarmed to Nelson from Donald and Revelstoke following the discoveries on Toad Mountain. The plant for the *Miner* was packed in by Joe Wilson's pack train from Sproat's Landing.

The first issue told the story of how Tom Brady stabbed Billy Gorman during an altercation over, of all things, a piece of bacon. On July 10, Ward Spinks, Nelson's first judge, presiding over Nelson's first criminal trial, sentenced Brady to 18 months at hard labour.

Meanwhile, the provincial government had allocated funds for public works in the Nelson area, and on July 7 a citizen's meeting was held in George Bigelow's store on Baker Street to discuss its distribution. During the meeting, a motion was put forth to set aside $200 for building a wharf.

This was supported by Nelson businessmen, but representatives of the Halls argued that a wharf was not needed. They claimed that goods had always been landed without a wharf, and that if one was needed, it would be built by the CPR. Stating that "the Halls had made the country," they threatened to withdraw their financial support completely if the entire amount of government funds was not used to construct a wagon road from Nelson to Toad Mountain, and they made it clear "they did not want a cumbrous committee to have anything to do with the matter." To that effect, one of the mine representatives moved an amendment to the motion, which, after some division, was passed.

M.S. Davys was then hired to survey the route, which started from the west end of Baker Street and crossed the old trail several times on route to the mines. A week later, Alfred Bunker, whose bid of $897 was the lowest of eight received, was awarded the contract for the first mile. The main sections of the road were to be 20 feet wide, while the roadbed on side hill cuttings was only required to be 12 feet. On August 2 the *Miner* reported that the first mile was nearly complete and bids for the remaining nine

*(Above) Eugene S. Topping.*
*(Right) The Tremont Hotel, Baker Street, Nelson, in 1891.*
*(Below) Judge William Ward Spinks presided over Nelson's first criminal trial in 1890.*

miles would be opened on August 4.

In early September, 2,000 sacks were ordered by the Hall mines to enable them to ship ore. By mid-month the tunnel on the Silver King was in over 200 feet, and was being driven at the rate of 12 to 13 feet a week. A new building was under construction, ore sorters were at work, and shipments averaging four tons a day were deposited at the Nelson waterfront. Joe Wilson, one of Nelson's best-known citizens, now had the contract for packing the ore. Six days a week his 24 pack animals made one round trip daily between the steamboat landing and the mine, delivering an estimated $1,000 to $1,200 worth or ore in 100 pound sacks. The *Surprise* and barge transported the ore from Nelson to Bonner's Ferry, making two trips a week.

On October 4, the *Miner* announced that the work on the wagon road had been temporarily suspended because the contractor was unable to complete the job at the contracted price. For a time the road committee was obliged to pay the men for their work by the day, but on October 25 the *Miner* announced that all work had cease with only three of the 10 miles completed. This was bad news, for, although the trail was in fair condition, there were steep sections that rose 1,000

feet to the mile. A week earlier, Wilson's pack train had brought down the last sack of the 2,500 shipped that year. Two months later, Wilson drowned in a freak accident on Kootenay Lake. It was a sad loss for Nelson, and the *Miner* devoted three-quarters of its front page to Wilson's life and the tragedy.

While there was very little news concerning the mine during the winter of 1890 and spring of 1891, the town of Nelson remained active. Four steamers plied between Nelson, Ainsworth, Balfour, Pilot Bay and Bonner's Ferry. The first steamboat to run on Kootenay Lake was William Baillie-Grohman's small screw-steamer *Midge*. She was brought in with great difficulty in 1884 to work on Grohman's reclamation project. The vessel eventually fell into the hands of T.L. Davis, after which it was known as the *Mud Hen*. The next steamer to make its appearance was the *Surprise*, which was put in service in 1885-86 by the Hendryx company operating the Bluebell mine. Following this came Fry's steamer *Idaho*, purchased from Captain Ainsley and Nelson Martin in the spring of 1888. Three months after the *Idaho* came the *Galena*, also owned by the Hendryx company. The *Galena* continued to be the principal boat on Kootenay Lake until June, 1891, when the *Nelson* was launched.

In addition, the C&K, a branch of the CPR, was being built between Nelson and Sproat, a small landing on the Columbia River 28 miles away. Sproat's Landing never amounted to anything more than a construction camp while workmen were building the line. In addition to the railway company's store, the only merchants were R.E. Lemon and Samuel Green. John A. Gibson ran a hotel there and Mrs. Schroeder conducted a restaurant. During construction of the grade in April, 1891, three men were killed in an explosion. Later that spring, the first regular train ran through. With the railway work finished, the residents of Sproat's Landing moved to Nelson. None of the original businessmen of Sproat's had purchased lots, and all of them moved without paying the owner, Thomas Sproat, anything in the way of rental. Some settled afterwards, but those who did not were sued.

The Nelson Electric Light Company was formed in 1891, but did nothing until 1896 when a system of house lighting was installed. 1891 also saw the formation of a fire company and the opening of telephone communications between various points on the lake. By now the town also had a public school and three churches.

On April 18, 1891, Toad Mountain once again made the news when the *Miner* reported "It is common rumor that an offer of $2,000,000 has been made for the Silver King, and that the offer is now being considered by the Halls and the Atkins estate interests." A week later the newspaper reported that the provincial government was about to resume work on the wagon road.

But the mine's rumoured sale remained the topic of interest when the Victoria *Colonist* reported on May 6: "There is a deposit of $150,000 in this city at the present time as a first payment of a total of $1,500,000 for the Silver King mine, on Toad Mountain, West Kootenay district. It is understood, however, that the owners, among whom are the heirs of the late Richard Day Atkins, will not consider any offer that is not well up in the millions."

Winslow Hall, who was in Nelson at the time, when shown the news despatch, commented: "If the Silver King has been sold I know nothing about it; and I guess I would know something about it if it were sold." Hall had been appointed superintendent of the wagon road, and by mid-May he had 40 men on site about to resume work. If everything went according to plans, he expected that machinery could be hauled over the road by July. As predicted, the road was completed that month at a total cost was $14,887.14, of which the Silver King contributed $4,000.

However, instead of producing and shipping ore, the Silver King settled into a development phase, and for a time, very little was reported on its activity. Then, in December, old rumours concerning its imminent sale resurfaced. This time the Silver King had been sold to a Scotch company for $1,000,000, of which the Hall interests were to receive half. These rumours were quashed on January 2, 1892, however, when the *Miner* reported that the Silver King mine had not been sold, and that its owners were expending more money in development work than any other management in the province, excepting the coal mines on Vancouver Island. By this time the tunnel was in over 800 feet.

While the uncertainty on Toad Mountain was continuing, Nelson itself was striding boldly ahead. On January 2, 1892, a branch of the Bank of Montreal was opened. The manager, A.H. Buchanan, had come in by way of Spokane a few days before on snowshoes, bringing with him the enormous capital of $11.50 with which to open the branch. In March of the same year the Bank of British Columbia opened under the management of A.F. Daly. Nelson's third bank was a private affair operated by Applewhaite & Allan in connection with their real estate business.

In April, H.E. Croasdale, who had spent the previous nine months in England, returned with the disappointing news that a buyer had not yet been found for the Silver King. As development work continued, absolutely no outsiders were permitted on the property. This secrecy kept the mine out of the limelight until mid-July, when the *Miner* announced that "Mr. Hall, accompanied by Mr. Macdonald, has gone to Scotland to be present at the final stages of the transfer of the Silver King property to a syndicate." At the same time, however, a Seattle newspaper announced that the sale of the mine was already a done deal, claiming it had been sold on July 2 for $2,000,000.

Once again, however, it was only wishful thinking. But still the rumours persisted, and in March, 1893, the Silver King once again made headlines when the *Miner,* quoting an eastern newspaper, reported that the mine had been sold for $1,800,000. Two weeks later the *Miner* was able to confirm the sale at last. Apparently a deal was reached in 1892, but had been held up when one of the biggest investors met with a fatal accident. This delayed the final transactions until the executors could work out the details. "The original holders of the mine have been bought out on a basis of half stock and half cash," reported the *Miner,* "the purchase price being $1,800,000. This will net each of the Hall interests $34,000 in cash, and a like amount in stock."

For some time the new company devoted itself almost entirely to development work, making extensive use of prospecting drills run by compressed air. The ground, surveyed to a depth of 1,000 feet below the surface, proved the continuing richness of the ore and led to a new policy regarding transportation in 1895.

After many trials and suggestions, a wire rope tramway known as the Hallidie system, manufactured by California Wire Works, was decided upon. (Mr. Hallidie was the builder of the famous suspension bridge across the Fraser River on the old Cariboo Road.)

The difficulties to contend with were by no means light. The survey for the tramway showed the distance to be four-and-a-half miles and the height of the mine 4,800 feet above Nelson. Crossing its line was the canyon of Giveout Creek which necessitated a long span without supports. All these troubles were overcome

*(Above) The Silver King tramway crew on Toad Mountain in 1896.*
*(Opposite page) The centre station of the tramway that hauled ore from the Silver*
*King mine on Toad Mountain to the smelter in Nelson, visible in the valley below.*
*(Inset) H.E. Croesdale.*

and when erected, the tramway was the largest Hallidie system in the world. It performed entirely by gravity, with the descending buckets full of ore hauling up the empty ones. But the strain proved too great. Four-and-a-half miles of buckets holding 100 pounds of ore each, hauling along a distance of almost a mile in sheer descent, was more than ordinary iron could stand. Thus the tramway was cut in two and a loading station installed halfway down. After this change was made the system carried down about 10 tons of ore an hour with complete satisfaction.

During the autumn of 1895 the Hall Mines smelter was erected under the supervision of Paul Johnson. The first furnace was blown in in January 1896, and with occasional intervals, worked until the erection of its enormous neighbour in August 1897. It was the largest in the northwest, if not the world, with a crucible measuring 144x54 inches and capable of producing 250 tons of ore a day.

At first the company was satisfied with turning out matte, containing some 48 or 49 percent of copper and silver. But during the summer of 1897 it put in a refinery consisting of reverberatory and roasting furnaces which produced blister copper containing 98 percent copper besides gold and silver. The first train load of this product was shipped by CPR to Montreal on route for Swansea where, by the electrolytic process, its valuable components of gold, silver and copper was further refined.

## NELSON HERITAGE BUILDINGS

1. NELSON COURT HOUSE. This building, designed by F.M. Rattenbury, was completed in 1909 at a cost of $109,146.
2. NELSON CITY HALL. Built in 1902 of Spokane pink brick and Kaslo marble, it originally served as a post office and customs house.
3. JOHN HOUSTON MEMORIAL. Erected in 1926 to honour Nelson's first mayor.
4. LAND REGISTRY OFFICE. Commissioned by Fred Hume, it was built of fire-retardant brick in 1899-1900.
5. McDONALD JAM FACTORY. Built in two parts. A two story frame structure was built in 1911 as a jam factory, and a stone warehouse was added in 1920.
6. BANK OF MONTREAL. Designed by F.M. Rattenbury and built in 1899-1900.
7. HAMILTON POWDER COMPANY. Built in 1895.
8. NELSON DAILY NEWS. Constructed in 1899-1900, it was sold to the Nelson *Daily News* in 1905.
9. BELLAMY'S GROCERY. Built c1895 and operated as a grocery store until 1972.
10. J.M. LUDWIG LEATHERGOODS. Built in 1897 for William Goepel, the building was soon used as a hardware, clothing and mining supplies store.
11. MAGLIO BLOCK. Built in 1914.
12. McKILLOP BUILDING. Built for Alexander McKillop, a mineral assayer, in 1897.
13. McCULLOCK BLOCK. Built in 1912.
14. MARA-BARNARD BLOCK. Built in 1897 as the first Royal Bank of Canada branch in the province.
15. STANDARD FURNITURE STORE. Built of locally fired brick in 1904.
16. BANK OF COMMERCE. Built in 1907 of Kootenay marble.
17. LAWRENCE'S HARDWARE STORE. Built in 1897, it was the first three storey building on Baker Street.
18. K.W.C. BLOCK. Kirpatrick, Wilson and Clements paid $10,500 for the building lots and built this block in 1901.
19. BURN'S BUILDING. Built in 1899 for millionaire "cattle king" Patrick Burns.
20. ABERDEEN BLOCK. First known as the Beer Block, it was built in 1898 by mine manager and hardware store owner George F. Beer.
21. HOUSTON BLOCK. Originally a bank, it was built in 1899.
22. EAGLES HALL. Built in 1909 of brick and trimmed with local granite, this building originally housed one of the finest dry goods and ladies wear stores in B.C.

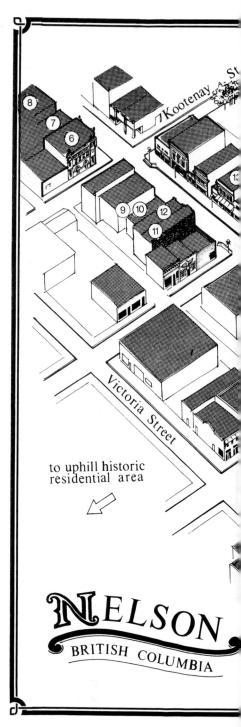

to uphill historic residential area

NELSON BRITISH COLUMBIA

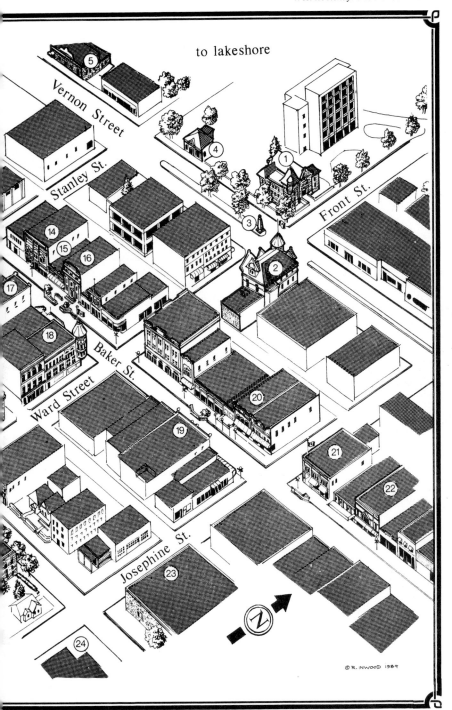

to lakeshore

Vernon Street

Stanley St.

Front St.

Baker St.

Ward Street

Josephine St.

© R. INWOOD 1984

*(Left) Richard A. Fry. He and his brother Martin were true pioneers in West Kootenay.*
*(Opposite page, top) Nelson's City Hall was constructed in 1902 of Spokane pink brick and Kaslo marble. It was originally used as a post office and customs house. In the right of photo is the monument to John Houston.*
*(Opposite page, inset) Nelson's first mayor, John Houston. Houston was also the publisher of the Donald Truth, 1888, and the Nelson Miner, 1890.*
*(Opposite page, bottom) A general view of the city of Nelson today.*

The Silver King mine was, for many years, one of the greatest producers in the Kootenays. It closed down in 1902, but was reopened occasionally until if shut down permanently in 1915. Below it, sprawled down Toad Mountain to the waterfront, was first the lusty camp known as Salisbury, then as the town of Stanley, which shortly became the City of Nelson.

Like every West Kootenay town, Nelson had its ups and downs, but it's long range prospects appeared bright. At one point it actually supported four newspapers.

During the winter of 1893-94, Daniel C. Corbin's Nelson & Fort Sheppard Railway (N&FS) was completed to Five Mile Point. It was forced to stop there because any further advance would encroach on land granted to the CPR. This obstacle was eventually resolved, however, and the N&FS built right into Nelson where it connected with the CPR.

In 1894 Nelson was struck by floods that devastated much of the province that year. During the previous winter the snowfall had been unusually heavy. This was followed by a balmy spring that continued uninterrupted into early summer. By May 24, Kootenay Lake had risen above its highest recorded level and was still rising. On June 3 a tremendous storm of wind, thunder and rain lashed the entire region. This melted the remaining snow and turned normally quiet streams into raging torrents, washing out bridges and railroad trestles.

The lake reached its peak on June 9. By that time the water stood six feet deep at the CPR depot. The town wharf was completely submerged and steamers were forced to land passengers among the shacks to the westward. A few days before the water reached its peak, the last train left the depot. It was not able to return for three months.

But Nelson survived, and in the spring of 1897 it was incorporated into a city. John Houston, who had founded Nelson's first newspaper, became the city's first mayor. Today, Nelson prides itself in the fact that it has more historic buildings than any other city or town in the province. ♣

# 4
# PIONEER DAYS IN
# WILD, WOOLLY YMIR

*Today, Ymir is a peaceful, law-abiding community nestled among the trees beside the Salmo River, 18 miles south of Nelson. But it was not always that way. During its heyday, Ymir was a tough mining town, with no limit poker games, drunken brawls, robberies, arson, suicide and even an occasional murder.*

T HE region first drew attention in the late 1850s when miners from the Pend D'Oreille River country began to move north in search of new placer creeks. Eventually they gravitated to the Salmon River area and began working tributaries like the North Fork, Hall, Wildhorse and Quartz. But when the early discoveries were exhausted, they deserted the area.

Interest was renewed when the Hall party made a rich silver discovery on Toad Mountain in the fall of 1886. Encouraged by their success, an old prospector named John Loge, accompanied by Sam McCaskill, ventured into the area. In a creek that emptied into Salmon River, they discovered coarse gold in shallow diggings, and a small rush followed. However, for some years, chiefly owing to the boom at Rossland, prospectors did not pay much attention to the area.

In the fall of 1891, Daniel Chase Corbin, the American railroad magnate, began to survey the route for his Nelson & Fort Sheppard Railway (N&FS). The 55-mile-long railway crossed the Pend D'Oreille River at Waneta, proceeded up the valley of Beaver Creek and followed the Salmon River to Nelson. During construction of the line, a water tank was erected at the mouth of Quartz Creek. This became a landmark for the surrounding country and was the objective point of prospectors searching for mineral wealth. A small hamlet known as Quartz Creek sprang up at the water tank and another at Salmon City, now Salmo, six miles south. By June 1893, there were upwards of 100 men scattered along the Salmon River and the prospects for the region looked bright. Ironically, Salmo, which was to enjoy a relatively peaceful history, had the dubious distinction of recording the first of numerous tragedies that would mar the area.

In October 1893, Steven Hamlin was playing cards in "an illicit whisky dive, kept by a man named Leslie" in Salmon City. A number of "notorious characters," including Charlie Ross, William O'Brien and Ruby McNair were also in the game, which proceeded without incident until midnight. But as the men rose from the table, Ross asserted that he had lost a cheque and demanded the right to search everyone. No one objected, but while Ross was searching Hamlin, O'Brien started for the door. Hamlin stopped him, words passed between the two, and Hamlin struck at O'Brien. Retaliating, O'Brien struck Hamlin twice and knocked him down, whereupon he proceeded to kick him in the head. A man named Sisson saw the first kick and interfered, but not before O'Brien had delivered another kick to Hamlin's head.

After a time Sisson and Leslie were able to partially revive Hamlin, but he was unable to stand on his feet. A bed was prepared and Sisson remained with Hamlin throughout the night. When his condition did not improve the next day it became evident he was not likely to live. At this point O'Brien and the others asked permission to take the wounded man into their tent to care for him. He was removed there, but "on Thursday the gang, consisting of Ross, O'Brien, McNair, and Leslie made tracks for the United States leaving their victim to die unattended. Hamlin died about midnight on Thursday."

Hamlin had been in Nelson a few days before his death and was known to possess a considerable amount of money. Likewise, he had been seen with a number of bank notes at the time of the assault, but no money of any description was found on him after death.

This murder, which seemed to set the tone for the lawlessness of the entire area, probably had a great deal to do with the isolation of the two camps. The United States border was only a short distance south of Salmo, while the only law enforcement was in Nelson, 24 miles north by crude trail.

In the spring of 1897, the area became the scene of renewed placer activity and over 100 claims were staked. On April 8, the old town-site of Quartz Creek was jumped by three Rossland men named Powell, Blake and Parker, who laid claim to 620 acres of ground.

The N&FS, which claimed the site by virtue of a government land grant, responded quickly, and on May 1 the Nelson *Miner* reported that Judge Angus J. McColl had issued a restraining order against the three Rossland men "enjoining them from proceeding with the survey of the land, pending the settlement of the case."

Two weeks later Corbin surveyed Quartz Creek and renamed the town-site Ymir (pronounced Y-mir). Lots were put on sale and in two days all the choice business lots were sold at prices ranging from $250 to $400. In all, 150 lots were sold with construction set to commence "in earnest as soon as the side track had been completed." Thus, Ymir became a siding for the N&FS.

In mid-June the Quartz Creek town-site case was heard in Nelson before Judge Walkem. During the trial, counsel for Parker, Powell and Blake alleged that the N&FS land grant had been given by the government on the stipulation that "a survey of the property be completed before the expiration of five years, and that this time had expired on April 8th without the survey having been made." On the surface, their claim appears valid, for, although the N&FS did obtain a six month extension, it was not obtained until after their five years had expired and after the three men had laid claim to the town-site. Nevertheless, Judge Walkem upheld the N&FS's claim to the property.

A week earlier, under the headline WILD, WOOLLY YMIR, the *Miner* related two stories that would underscore the lawless nature of the town for much of its frontier history.

In the middle of the night, R.A. Chisholm, proprietor of the Kootenay Hotel at Ymir, was awakened by Malcolm McDonald, one of his lodgers, entering the room. McDonald demanded money he claimed the hotel-man owed him. When Chisholm denied owing him money, McDonald raised a rifle to fire. Chisholm ducked just as

*(Above) An early scene at Salmo. Despite starting its career with a murder, Salmo settled into a relatively quiet community.*
*(Opposite page) A general view of Ymir in 1984 showing the Ymir Hotel and the Palace Hotel.*
*(Opposite page, left inset) The Hotel Ymir.*
*(Opposite page, right inset) The Cosmopolitan Hotel in Ymir in 1898.*
*(Below) The Salmo Hotel as it looks today. It's outward appearance has not changed since it was built.*

the bullet passed over his head and through the clothing which was hanging on the bed post.

When Chisholm reported the incident to Nelson authorities, Constable Wolverton immediately started out for Ymir. A few days earlier Dave Keefe, proprietor of the Windsor Hotel, had come into Nelson for the purpose of having one J. Condon arrested. He said Condon had ejected him from his own hotel and had taken forcible possession. When the constable arrived there, Condon had disappeared. McDonald, however, was not as fortunate. Apprehended, he was sent up for trial, and on June 28 was sentenced by Judge Walkem to five years at hard labour in the penitentiary.

Ymir's rowdiness made the news less than a year later when, on May 11, 1898, L.W. Teneyck and Peter McKay were arrested for robbing a dead man of $100 and a gold watch. The two men had been with James Chisholm when he died earlier in the week. The following day, Teneyck and McKay were "flush of money, one of them coming out in a new suit of clothes, and the other was filling up with 'Johnnie Alcohol'." Tried on May 13, Teneyck and McKay received sentences of five and six months respectively.

By this time Ymir's population was about 1,000 and growing. Producing mines with big payrolls made Corbin's little town a booming centre, and by 1900 it boasted 80 buildings, including nine hotels: Miller, Ross, Ymir, McLeod, Vancouver, Palace, Waldorf, St. Charles and Cosmopolitan. It also had a brewery that advertised "drink our beer and you will agree that you want nothing better." Other establishments included four general stores, three barber shops, a drug store, a book store, a branch of the Merchants Bank of Halifax, a weekly newspaper, Methodist and Presbyterian churches, an excellent public school with 40 pupils in daily attendance, a doctor, lawyer, mining broker's office, butcher, bakery, post office, assayer and a hospital.

The first of three weekly newspaper, the Ymir *Miner* probably made its appearance in 1898. In July of that year, it commented on the potential of the mining town:

"Ymir has the brightest future of any mining camp in British Columbia. There are at present eight or 10 properties working, and a good number of them will put in machinery during the summer and fall. There are at present two concentrators and three stamp mills under construction, all of which will be completed within the next few months. . . . There are at present 200 men at work on the different properties around Ymir, and placing the wages of these men at $3.50 per day, regular miner's wages, this would at present give Ymir a payroll of $21,000 per month."

A few months later the paper was sold to A.L. Knox, a newspaper man from South Africa. Its success was short-lived, however, for when the Ymir *Mirror,* published by C. Dell-Smith, made its appearance in 1901, the Ymir *Miner* had already departed the scene. By this time gold bricks worth $40,000 were turned out monthly, and for a brief period the Ymir was the largest gold mine in the British Empire.

Ymir had enjoyed almost four years of relative tranquillity when, on February 6, 1904, the *Mirror* published some improprieties concerning the Ymir General Hospital. For some time the *Mirror* had been receiving request from its readers for information "as to the inner workings of the institution." These readers had tried without success to get answers from the hospital board, and when the paper ran into a similar roadblock, they decided to investigate.

The hospital was mainly funded by the provincial government and private subscriptions, which included medical fees of $1 per month deducted from the pay of mine employees. After being refused a copy of the monthly report forwarded to the government, the newspaper obtained a copy from Victoria. Examination of the report revealed some apparent irregularities: the hospital expenses appeared to be exaggerated, while the revenue seemed to be understated. The *Mirror* also found it odd that although "Almost every entertainment got up in Ymir during the term covered by these figures, were in aid of the hospital, yet the only credit given is $10 attributed to 'other sources'." The *Mirror* showed the report to several parties interested in the hospital and the general verdict was "mysterious," prompting Smith to state that "The accounts will stand investigation." By bringing this matter to light, however, the *Mirror* was pointing an accusing finger at the Ymir Miners' Union, "who claimed the exclusive right of running the hospital."

This was not the first time the *Mirror* had clashed with the union, and a few days after the article appeared, Smith received a visit from the union leaders who threatened his paper with a boycott. Instead of backing down, Smith fought back with a biting editorial in his next edition: "What a pity that a trades' union — founded on sound principals — should be dominated by 'have-beens' while the practical working members are pursuing their honorable avocation! If this little clique of fanatics could only have their way life in Ymir would be intolerable and things would be made so hot that capital would give the camp a wide berth. . . . In the interests of the public we gave publicity to figures showing how the receipts of the Ymir General Hospital are handled, and for this heinous offence the merchants of town are to be ORDERED by the little clique to withdraw their patronage from the *Mirror,* under the usual dire penalties."

In its February 20 issue, the *Mirror,* under the bold heading "WAR IN YMIR!" reported that the union had followed through on its threatened boycott and published a list of storekeepers and saloon men who had surrendered "to the threats of the tyrants." Flying in the face of adversity, the paper published additional information pertaining to the questionable activities of the union, ending the article by stating "We have the honor of being the first newspaper boycotted in British Columbia."

The following week the *Mirror* placed the normal ads of the boycotting businesses upside down and sideways around a large headstone which read: "Erected to the departed spirit of Ymir business men, by the Boycott Committee, February, A.D., 1904, *Requiescat in Pace.*" On another page in the same issue a large ad read: "Send the *Mirror* to your friends and help advertise the camp as it is today. There is no more effective means of accomplishing this end. Caution them to avoid the place as they would a plague. Ymir is in the grasp of a band of demagogues who are making life intolerable. Boycotting is their present form of persecuting those who will not yield to their sway. Let your friends know the true state of affairs and send them a copy of the *Mirror.*"

Although the boycott was clearly hurting the paper, to its credit it did not yield, and starting with its March 5 issue it added the words "Published in the Boycotting Camp of British Columbia" in large letters under its front page masthead. The same issue revealed than more businesses had withdrawn their advertising support.

Near the end of March, Ymir's lawlessness again took centre stage, and for a brief time grabbed the spotlight from the newspaper's boycott.

The incident began on Sunday, March 20, 1904. Murdoch Campbell was talking

(Above) A general view of Ymir's main business section. The Hotel Ymir can be seen just above boxcar in lower right. The Palace is just behind it, while behind and to the left of the Palace Hotel is St. Anne's Church. All three buildings stand today.
(Opposite page, top left) Services are still conducted in St. Anne's Church every other Sunday.
(Opposite page, top right) Dr. E.C. Arthur, of Nelson, conducted the inquiry into McDermid's death.
(Opposite page, centre) The Nelson & Fort Sheppard train at Ymir.
(Opposite page, bottom) Remains of the Ymir Gold Mines Ltd. Stamp Mill across the Salmo River from Ymir.
(Below) The Palace Hotel in Ymir in August 1984. Still being lived in today, the hotel is for sale.

to some friends in the Cosmopolitan Hotel when Alexander McDermid, another miner, barged into the group and began to taunt Campbell. Campbell realized that McDermid was drunk, and left the hotel to avoid a confrontation.

When the two men met again on the main street of Ymir on Monday morning, McDermid's animosity had apparently calmed down, for the two men exchanged "good mornings." However that evening, when the two men met in the bar of the Ymir Hotel, McDermid, who had been doing some serious drinking, demanded two bits from Campbell.

When Campbell replied that he didn't have the money, McDermid took off his coat and assumed a boxing stance. Flailing about with his fists, he boasted: "I can lick both of you Campbells." Then, glancing at another miner standing nearby, he said: "Murdie, you know that you are nothing but a damned cur."

Neither man wanted any trouble with McDermid, who had been known to use a knife in previous fights. Leaving the hotel, Campbell crossed the street to the Cosmopolitan, where he stayed for a time to talk to some friends.

Later, as Campbell was leaving the Cosmopolitan for home, he had the misfortune of encountering his old nemesis in front of the Ymir Hotel. After a brief argument, McDermid swung at Campbell. In his drunken stupor, he apparently missed. Campbell responded and McDermid went down in the snow.

Herbert McNeill and three others had witnessed the incident from the Cosmopolitan Hotel and had seen somebody fall. Not wishing to become involved, however, they ducked back into the hotel. A few minutes later, McNeill, curious about the outcome of the fight, emerged from the Cosmopolitan. Crossing the street, he found McDermid lying on his back, bleeding and unconscious, choking in his own blood. While a couple of men carried the injured man into the Cosmopolitan, McNeill ran to fetch the doctor. But by the time he arrived, McDermid was dead.

On March 22, Dr. Edward C. Arthur of Nelson, chief coroner of the district, arrived in Ymir to conduct an enquiry into the death. During the inquest McNeill testified that, just before the tragic encounter, he had seen McDermid in the Ymir Hotel. "He was intoxicated and threatening to lick Campbell, who was sitting in an armchair in the Ymir barroom." McNeill later left the hotel and went across the street to the Cosmopolitan. A short time later he saw Campbell enter.

McNeill later left the Cosmopolitan, and while talking with three others on the street outside, they were joined by Campbell. After a brief conversation, during which Campbell stated that he could not stand McDermid's abuse much longer, Campbell left the group and walked some distance along the street. When he reached the street crossing, Campbell met another man McNeill assumed was McDermid. McNeill testified that he heard loud talking and cursing, then one man fell. However, since it was dark, and the two men were 90 feet away, McNeill could not say if any blows had been struck. At this point, not wanting to get involved, McNeill and the other men went back into the Cosmopolitan Hotel. However McNeill knew McDermid to be a dangerous man, so after about five minutes he decided to investigate. When he arrived at the scene he found McDermid lying on his back and bleeding badly. Campbell was nowhere in sight.

The coroner queried McNeill: "While you were in the Cosmopolitan, had you an idea that the fight was still going on outside?"

"I did not know," McNeill replied. "But I was uneasy, for McDermid had the reputation of being a dangerous man." He paused, then added, "Handy with a knife, too." In answer to a question from one of the jurors, he replied, "Yes, I thought Campbell was trying to avoid McDermid." Another question brought the reply, "When I saw McDermid fall, I judged it was from a blow of a man's hand. I did not see any weapon with Campbell."

The coroner then asked, "Have you any idea why Campbell went back near the Ymir if he wished to avoid McDermid?"

McNeill replied that he did not know. "I could not say that Campbell was under the influence of liquor." In answer to yet another question from Arthur, he replied, "When Campbell came over to talk to us in the Cosmopolitan, he said he had left the Ymir because he was afraid McDermid would hit him with a chair."

Dr. Duncan then presented evidence as to the nature of the wounds. "There was a cut at the corner of the left eye. The nose was broken. There was a deep cut right across the right corner of the chin an inch and a half long."

Upon removing the top of the skull during the post-mortem examination, a large quantity of blood rushed out through the cut. The blood vessels of the brain were greatly congested. Although there was no fracture of the skull, there was laceration or tearing of the brain. In all other respects, however, the brain was normal.

Dr. Duncan stated that the cause of death was due "...to pressure of the blood extravasated into the cranium and also to the great congestion of the vessels of the brain." He further stated that he knew McDermid personally, and considered him "...a likely subject for apoplexy." Asked to give his opinion as to how the wounds were inflected, Dr. Duncan would not hazard a guess, stating only that the most critical wound above the right temple "might have been caused by falling on a hard substance."

Although warned by the coroner that his statement could be used against him, Murdoch Campbell volunteered his story. After detailing the abuses he suffered from McDermid that Sunday and Monday, Campbell stated: "I did not want trouble with the man, for I knew he used a knife. I left the Ymir Hotel and crossed over to the Cosmopolitan. Then I started back and was going down to the Ross house and then on home. I met the deceased at the crossing and he struck at me. I struck at him and knocked him down. I struck him twice after he fell and I walked off and left him. I went down to the Ross house, and washed the blood from my hands, and sat there awhile. I then went up to the Cosmopolitan and the deceased was lying on the floor. I walked around town until I heard McDermaid (sic) was dead and then I went and gave myself up to the police. I struck McDermaid with my fist. I had nothing but my bare knuckles."

"Did you kick him?" asked the coroner.

"I don't know," Campbell replied. "I might have. I was mad at the time and did not know what I was doing. I never had a quarrel with him before."

This closed the evidence and, after a brief consultation, the jury returned a verdict that "...Alexander McDermid came to his death at Ymir, B.C., on Monday, March 21st, as the results of blows inflicted by Murdoch Campbell," who, at 18 years of age, was then arrested and sent to Nelson for trial.

Shortly after 3 p.m. on March 23, the coffin containing McDermid's remains was placed on a woodrack sleigh and, followed by a Presbyterian parson and one friend of the deceased, was driven to the potter's field at the cemetery. A hitch occurred at the cemetery when three men realized they could not handle the lowering of McDermid, a big man of 215 pounds, into his grave by themselves. They had to

(Above) The Ymir Gold Mines Ltd. Stamp Mill across the Salmo River from Ymir.

(Right) The headstone of Murdoch Campbell in the Quartz Creek (Ymir) Cemetery in October 1985. The inscription reads: "Murdc Campbell, died Oct. 20, 1912, Aged 26 years. Native of Harris, Scotland. Erected by his brothers."

(Opposite page) The remains of the Ymir Gold Mines Ltd. Stamp Mill in 1984.

(Below) A panoramic view of Ymir in 1984.

send back to the town for help.

That same day, at a preliminary investigation held before Percy J. Gleazer, JP, witnesses attested to Campbell's lawyer that his client was a peaceable, law-abiding man, while McDermid was a very dangerous character. No one testified on behalf of the dead man.

The editor of the *Mirror,* however, came to the defence of the deceased, claiming, "He had many good traits of character." Smith also used the opportunity to rekindle the boycotting issue by charging that the union not only boycotted living people, but also boycotted the dead by not allowing people to attend the funeral.

During the investigation, Constable Forrester demonstrated some black humour when he asked one of the witnesses: "Did the blow sound like the stroke of a man's fist or the noise of a crosscut saw?"

Editor Smith seized upon this insensitivity as being typical of the man, and went after the constable in his newspaper. He wrote: "The camp is fast becoming one of the most lawless in the Wild and Wolly (sic) West, and will continue to enjoy this most unenviable reputation until it is properly policed. . . The camp always had a reputation, but it is getting worst. . . Any crime that does not call for the services of the undertaker may be settled out of court for a monetary consideration, and with the full knowledge and acquiescence of the local policeman. The evildoers know this and act accordingly. . .most of these grievous assault cases have their origin in one or other of the nine barrooms which disgrace the camp or in some of the red-light establishments across the stream. (Ymir's other main street was across the Salmo River.) When a crime is committed, somebody had to hunt up the constable and give him the details, and then settlement is in order. In the little incident of Monday evening the man who killed the other was obliged to hunt up Forrester and give himself up — instead of Forrester hunting him up. Forrester is the man who is suppose to do the police work here."

The crusading editor was not impressed with the constable's patrolling of the saloons either: "Yet these are the licensed premises which year after year Forrester certifies as being orderly and well conducted."

He continued his attack: ". . .McDermid bleeding and unconscious on the roadside. The dead body is removed to the hospital, and thence to the undertaker's. . . The first thought that would strike even an unexperienced policeman would be to make a thorough search of the ground for the weapon, if any, used in killing. Such a notion, however, never dawned in the mind of Forrester. A man had been killed, and some accident would bring evidence his way. This did not turn up until Thursday morning, when a bloodstained knife was accidentally discovered in the snow at the exact spot where the dead body was found. A boy found it. Now, according to the doctor's evidence, there were some nasty cuts on the dead man's face. Campbell went into the Ross House 'to wash the blood from his hands.' But Forrester does not seem to see the connection. The man is worst than useless in the camp as a police constable, and that the department does not tumble to the fact is not at all creditable. It is lamentable that Ymir should be notorious for its lawlessness."

After being incarcerated for two months in the Provincial Goal at Nelson, the trial of Murdoch Campbell began on May 10, 1904. The presiding judge had read the case against Campbell the night before and it was his opinion that no case could be made against him.

The prosecutor argued briefly that there was evidence of a motive on the part of the accused. There was, he claimed, also evidence to show that Campbell went back to meet with McDermid, and he reminded the court that the prisoner had stated at the time that he "could not stand McDermid's treatment much longer" and shortly after, the encounter occurred.

Witnesses Roberts, McNeill and Clark could not agree for sure whether or not Campbell had gone out of his way to meet McDermid, or just happened upon him on his (Campbell's) way home. Finally the judge advised the jury that, as a matter of law, the evidence offered by the Crown would not justify them in finding a verdict against the accused. It was then their duty to return a formal verdict. Through their foreman they did — not guilty.

Campbell was then discharged. A moment later he was being congratulated by his brothers and friends, who were in waiting, and the Ymir homicide case was a thing of the past.

Murdoch Campbell continued to live in the area for the rest of his life, which, tragically, was not long. On October 20, 1912, at the age of 26, he was killed in a landslide outside the Queen mine at Sheep Creek, 10 miles from Salmo. Campbell was buried in the Quartz Creek (Ymir) Cemetery, where his brothers erected a classic Scottish headstone in his memory. Elsewhere in the cemetery, the location unknown, lies the remains of Alexander McDermid.

Meanwhile, the boycott against the *Mirror* was seriously effecting its operation. By April 9, 1904, it had shrunk to a single page, a size it maintained until April 30, when it ceased publication altogether. The union had won; they had defeated the voice of a free press because it had dared to criticize its questionable activities. Three weeks later a new paper, *The Ymir Herald,* made its appearance, its four pages filled with advertising from the same businesses who had boycotted the *Mirror.*

Five months later, on November 1, 1904, most of Ymir's main business block was destroyed by fire. Members of the fire brigade were on the scene promptly and they later claimed they could have contained the fire quickly with comparatively little damage, but the hose nozzles were unaccountably missing. After a frantic search they were discovered under the *Herald* printing office. The half-hour delay proved costly, however, allowing the flames time to destroy most of the southern buildings on the block.

The principal loss occurred to T.H. Atkinson's drug store, where the fire was thought to have originated. Destruction of his store and contents amounted to $12,000, $8,000 of which was insured. Other heavy losers included the McVicar building (half drug store) $1,000; Seaney's general stock valued at $8,000, uninsured; the McCorquodale building valued at $1,500, uninsured; Newitt's dry goods stock valued at $8,000, $3,000 of which was insured, and the Coffey building, barber shop, and household effects, valued at $2,000, half of which was insured.

In view of the mysterious circumstances of the fire, suspicion fell upon Atkinson and a search warrant was obtained for his private residence. Based upon the evidence found there, Atkinson was arrested.

At a preliminary trial on November 4, Constable Fraser testified that he first heard the fire alarm at about 1:40 a.m., and by the time he arrived on the scene the fire was burning the rear end of Atkinson's drug store and the post office. The hose was then connected to the fire hydrant but the nozzles were missing and nothing could be done. The following morning he obtained a search warrant and searched Atkinson's private residence. In the basement he was shown a number of boxes containing druggist supplies and was told that was all there was. However, further investigation found more boxes concealed under some rubbish in a corner and on sills below the floor. He was again told there wasn't any more.

The next day, while Atkinson was in Nelson, Fraser returned with Gleazer and found a second cache of goods under the veranda. Later, in company with Kearns and Gleazer, a third cache was found. Subsequently he found other caches and estimated that the total quantity of all the goods discovered would cover 20 square feet of floor space.

A picture was beginning to emerge that Atkinson had been removing stock from his store in deliberate anticipation of setting it on fire for the insurance. This scenario was strengthened by Seaney when he testified that a show case that normally contained expensive goods had been replaced by toilet paper, and that advertisements were hung on shelves to hide the empty spaces. Seaney concluded his testimony by estimating that the store's stock had been reduced by two thirds prior to the fire.

Harry Kearns, who occupied the top floor of the Atkinson's building, added more damning evidence when he testified that he had grown suspicious that Atkinson might be planing a fire and had, on October 24, so notified the police.

Insurance agent E.B. McDermid, of Nelson, testified to writing a $4,000 insurance policy on Atkinson's stock on March 19, 1904. Gleazer testified that he had been unaware of this $4,000 policy when he insured the stock for $1,500 two days later.

Defence witness Archibald Bremner testified that he and Watts were first on the scene. When they arrived, the fire was entirely behind Seaney's store, and he saw no fire behind the post office or Atkinson's drug store. Fred Philbert collaborated Bremner's testimony by stating he saw Seaney's roof fall first, then Coffey's and lastly Atkinson. R.A. Ibbotson also swore positively to seeing no fire in Atkinson's store or the post office when he arrived; it was confined to the rear of Seaney's store.

When Atkinson took the stand he testified that at the time of the fire he had fully $10,000 worth of goods in the store, less what he had taken home, which he estimated to be worth $700. As for removing goods, he said he did this every year to prevent certain items from freezing during the cold winter. This was acknowledged by Sidney Ross of Salmo, who testified that he had known Atkinson in former years to carry stock home and store it in his cellar.

The evidence, all of which was circumstantial, was sufficient for the judge to remand Atkinson for arson at the spring assizes in Nelson. The strain of these accusations had their effect on Atkinson. He broke down completely at one point while testifying, and he fainted when the judge rendered his decision. However, the stress was to have far more tragic consequences for Mrs. Atkinson.

On March 23, 1905, the Nelson *Economist* reported: "Mrs. T.H. Atkinson, of Ymir, wife of the druggist who awaits trial on a charge of arson, committed suicide by drowning herself in the Ymir reservoir Thursday afternoon, while laboring under great mental strain. Shortly before committing the act, she took off her rings, and placing them in a chamois bag, said to her little eight-year-old girl: 'Gladys, in case anything happens to mamma, wear these around your neck.' Then she proceeded to the reservoir and swallowing a dose of poison, threw herself in."

The *Economist* concluded its article by stating: "Truly the women of Ymir are to be congratulated on their display of exclusiveness. Here was a woman most unfortunately situated, and just at the time when she should reasonably have counted on the sympathy of her neighbours she was shunned by her own sex."

What made the suicide even more tragic was the fact that Atkinson was acquitted of the charges at his trial less than two months later.

Although Ymir was rebuilt after the fire, it never achieved the prosperity it had previously enjoyed. During the First World War most of the mines in the area shut down. They were reopened in the 1930s and 1940s when the price of gold was high.

Today, of Ymir's nine original saloons, only the historic Ymir Hotel remains standing and still operating. People still occupy the crumbling Palace Hotel, but the stately St. Charles, sadly, was demolished several years ago. On the top of the hill at the end of a street, St. Anne's Church still stands. Services are conducted here every other Sunday. And surrounding it all stands Ymir, alone with the memories of gambling joints, saloons, outlaws and the cold, hard reality of work in the mines. ♣

*(Left) E.B. McDermid of Nelson c1908. He testified that he sold $4,000 worth of insurance to Atkinson six months before the fire.*
*(Below) The Presbyterian Church and Manse in Ymir, c1898.*

# 5
# ROSSLAND:
# THE GOLDEN CITY

*Known far and wide as "The Golden City," Rossland produced more gold than the combined placer creeks and rivers of B.C. The king of the hill, the legendary LeRoi, alone produced nearly $30,000,000.*

I N 1887, Leyson and Brohman, two prospectors from Rock Creek, noticed an outcrop along the trail and staked the Lily May, the first link in a chain of events which was to lead to the discovery of Red Mountain. The Lily May, however, seemed unpromising and was allowed to lapse, only to be re-staked in 1889 by Newlin Hoover and Oliver Bordeaux. In the spring of 1890, an American prospector from Colville appeared on the scene to do assessment work on the claim. His name was Joe Moris, and little did he suspect that within the year, he would be responsible for changing the tranquil face of the tree covered basin into a booming gold camp.

When the owners of the Lily May did not pay Moris for his assessment work, he decided to prospect on his own. Intrigued by the hill on the opposite side of the little valley, he struck out to investigate the red mountain. But the greater prize eluded him, for on the way there he came across a good showing of ore and stopped to locate a mineral claim which he named the Home Stake. Soon out of money and low on supplies, Moris set out for Nelson to replenish both. Later in the spring he returned to resume work on his claim in the Trail Creek basin.

A short time later two more prospectors turned up and began to scout the vicinity. One soon quit in disgust, but the other, Joe Bourgeois, remained and joined up with Moris as a partner.

As spring wore on and turned to summer, they edged their way closer to the beckoning slopes of the red mountain and by July 1 they were prospecting a narrow gulch on its eastern flank. Showings in the draw were numerous and rich looking, and it was soon apparent that the entire region was highly mineralized. On July 2 they staked four claims: the War Eagle, Centre Star, Idaho and Virginia. Under provincial mining law each man was allowed to hold only two claims, but despite this, Moris decided to stake off an extension on the Centre Star. He called this claim the LeWise.

When the prospectors arrived at the government office in Nelson, they offered the LeWise to Eugene S. Topping, the agent, if he would pay the $12.50 filing fee on all five claims. Topping agreed, and on July 7, the first four claims were recorded. Topping recorded his claim 10 days later, having decided in the meantime to rename it the LeRoi. The claims of Moris and Bourgeois stimulated interest in the area, and by August 2, there were 19 locations in the Trail Creek district.

R.E. Lemon, who recorded the Josie, applied for permission to purchase 320 acres of land on the east side of the Columbia and 160 acres on the west side. Meanwhile, Topping also had an application in for 200 acres on the west side. Two weeks later Lemon reported that there were "about 40 men scattered about the hills over there. There is a good restaurant at the mouth of the (Trail) creek, some 8 miles from the mines, and no lack of supplies." This restaurant was probably the one owned by a Mr. Poulton at the stopping place near the landing.

In the first week of September, Lemon, who had sacked 600 pounds of ore from his claim and shipped it to Spokane Falls, reported that he received $60 in gold and $2.50 in silver. This was to be far exceeded by Topping's LeRoi claim, however, as the Nelson *Miner* reported on September 27: "The assays rather astonished the owner, they being the best in the camp, the highest being $217 in gold to the ton." Topping then went to Spokane where he sold his mine to a syndicate for $35,000. Returning to Trail Creek, he promptly established a two-story hotel he named the Trail House, prempted a town-site and went into real estate.

Meanwhile, the syndicate registered the property as the LeRoi Mining and Smelting Company of Spokane. An inclined shaft was sunk and the initial assays were astonishing! The ore ran from three to 10 ounces in silver, five to 20 percent copper, and from $48 to $470 per ton in gold.

This first real strike caused a considerable stir in mining circles but almost immediately various difficulties were encountered; it was impossible to transport ore, even rich ore, profitably over mountain trails. The cost of supplies was also heavy and development work slow and difficult. To compound matters, after the initial strike at the LeRoi, the other properties failed to find significant ore bodies. An option on the War Eagle was dropped and the Centre Star was not proving up as expected.

Nevertheless, by 1892, a camp was gradually building up and one of the early arrivals, Ross Thompson, had the foresight to preempt 160 acres of land for a town-site. In that same year a wagon road was completed to Northport in Washington state and the LeRoi Company, now confident of the future, ordered 40 heavy wagons to transport their ore to that town where it would be transshipped to Helena, Montana, for smelting.

Growing pains had been experienced during the first two years, but in 1893 the camp started to come into its own when, early in the year, the LeRoi struck it again — this time a huge body of high grade ore.

Boomers, stock promoters, gambling men, dance hall girls and the usual assortment of drones of the frontier camps began drifting in. Soon a motley collection of cheap, ramshackle false front buildings, cabins and shacks sprang up on a crooked little street at the south end of Centre Star gulch. This new haven was soon dubbed "Sourdough Alley."

In that same year a wagon road east to Trail Creek Landing was completed and with it came easier access to the mines and a decrease in the cost of supplies.

Through the next year the town grew gradually as the LeRoi became a steady shipper. The prestige of the camp increased again when it was announced that F. Augustus Heinze, the 24-year-old millionaire mining genius from Butte, Montana, intended to build a smelter at Trail Creek Landing to treat the Rossland ores. He also proposed to build a tramway to carry the ore from Rossland to the smelter.

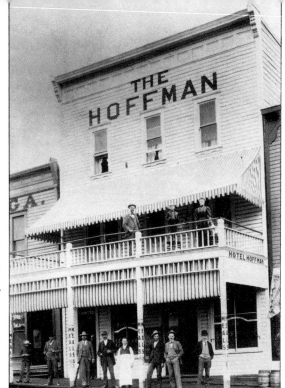

(Above) Joseph Moris. The discoveries he made with partner Joe Bourgeois led to a stampede to Red Mountain and the founding of Rossland. When this photo was taken in 1959, Moris was 95 years of age.
(Right) The Hoffman House, Rossland, B.C., c1905.
(Below) A squatter's cabin built of bark at Rossland.

The news of the great Heinze moving into the camp allayed the fears of many doubters and a shining future seemed assured.

Early in 1895, the camp rocketed to fame when the War Eagle struck a massive chute of exceptionally rich ore and then, at virtually the same time, the Centre Star drifted across a magnificent high grade vein. Soon, news of strikes at other properties rolled in as the Black Bear, Josie, Nickle Plate, Iron Mask and a number of other mines in the vicinity encountered good values. The golden era had begun!

The population jumped from 300 to over 3,000 and as the business section outgrew Sourdough Alley, it spilled over into Ross Thompson's new town-site. The railroad giants; Corbin's Northern Pacific (NPR), Hill's Great Northern (GNR) line and Shaughnessy's Canadian Pacific (CPR) now began to manoeuvre into position to challenge Heinze, the Montana upstart. A regular stage began running in March of 1895 as the company of Ashcroft, Seal & Gillies put 10-passenger Concords onto their Rossland-Trail Creek Landing run. The sound of staking echoed through the nearby hills and by the end of that year, 1,997 claims had been recorded where there had been only 99 two years before.

By 1896, the town had taken on a definite cosmopolitan air as the new three story Rossland Club came into being. In its plush surroundings, individuals like F.A. Heinze, General Warren and Oliver Durant gathered to promote present schemes or plot future ones. Along Columbia Avenue, now acknowledged as the main thoroughfare, hotels, stores and other businesses appeared almost daily.

Down Sourdough Alley and crowded Columbia Avenue strode legions of boomers, tinhorns, prospectors, women of easy virtue and hosts of others. Along with the usual assortment of real estate salesmen, stock promoters, mining magnets and other legitimate businessmen who flocked to the new bonanza, came the less desirable element — drifters, gamblers, and petty criminals — the riffraff of the camps who were always attracted to boom towns where easy money was to be made.

The appointment of John Kirkup as peace officer in Rossland at this time was providential. For months the camp had been gaining a name for lawlessness. In the dozens of saloons along Columbia Avenue, and the more notorious Sourdough Alley, scores of ne'er-do-wells lurched drunkenly from establishment to establishment, often fully armed and spoiling for a fight.

One particularly gory crime had been committed just prior to Kirkup's arrival in Rossland, when a smouldering dispute between two inhabitants of Sourdough Alley suddenly erupted into a bloody battle. When the smoke had cleared, Hugh McLaughlin lay dead, the bloody victim of repeated blows from an axe wielded by his brutal adversary, a certain James Westgate. The murderer was subsequently arrested, given over to trial in Nelson and sentenced to a mere 11 months imprisonment by a sympathetic jury. It was an ominous sign, and one which did not escape the attention of officials in Victoria. Rossland, it appeared, was threatening to become a wide open camp like many of the mining camps in the Coeur d'Alene country of Idaho or Montana, which were notorious for their lawlessness. Kirkup, they felt, would balance the scales.

And balance the scales he did. A gargantuan figure, six-feet-three-inches tall and weighing nearly 300 pounds, Kirkup had been an experienced peace officer for over 15 years. He was 40 years old, in his prime, and had faced some of the toughest cases in the west, from gunman to tinhorns, from whisky peddlers to smugglers, and he had never been backed down. But Rossland was different from any other place he had ever been in. It was predominantly an American camp. Nearly 80 percent of its inhabitants were Americans, used to that peculiar brand of frontier justice known as "miner's" law.

Gradually, Kirkup began to mould Rossland into "his town." Sidearms were strictly forbidden and had to be deposited for safekeeping upon entering the city limits. Kirkup himself had discarded his Colt, relying instead on a shot-loaded billy that had reputedly been given to him by an Idaho convict. It proved to be a deceptively lethal weapon in the hands of Kirkup.

Although Kirkup's reign in Rossland was only 16 months, the anecdotes about his exploits during that tenure are innumerable. He was somewhat inclined to settle disputes in an arbitrary manner. In fact, when he was the law in Rossland, few cases reached the courts. In some instances his remedies were a little crude. On one occasion a squatter insisted upon building near a stream in Sourdough Alley. This was not in keeping with the general understanding that nobody built near a stream; a common sense rule which protected the water supply. Kirkup, upon hearing that the new arrival was ignoring the usual custom, walked over to have a look at the situation. After a short exchange between the burly lawman and the equally adamant squatter, Kirkup simply put his shoulder to the shack and pushed the whole business into the creek. Wordlessly he walked away leaving behind the open-mouthed offender. It was an example of "Kirkup's Law." It would not have stood up in a court of law, but it was understood and respected in a mining camp.

On another occasion, when he was walking his beat, he heard an uproar emanating from Spellman's Saloon. This was followed by a volley of shots. Kirkup broke through the door of the saloon and immediately saw that a high stakes poker game had come apart at the seams, and the players were about to settle their differences

*(Above) Ross Thompson. In 1892 he preempted 160-acre for a town-site. At first known as Thompson's, it later became Rossland.*

*(Left) Const. James Kirkup, c1894, was appointed peace officer for Rossland in 1896.*

*(Right) An early view of Columbia Avenue, Rossland.*

with lead. Without a moment's hesitation he waded in with his loaded billy. When the fracas was over Kirkup was in sole possession of the premises, had collected the forbidden hardware and sent the gunmen packing.

The lawman's admirers were many. It was common knowledge that all the professional fights in Rossland "were on the square" while Kirkup was there, even when they were held in the infamous International House. Finally, however, Kirkup was dethroned by his old Achilles heel, his dislike of politicians. In this case it happened to be the newly elected mayor of Rossland, Col. Robert Scott, a long-time politician who made it clear from the outset that Kirkup's days were numbered. In July, 1897, Kirkup was relieved of his duties and replaced with J.S. Ingraham. The provincial government, however, soon appointed Kirkup as Government Agent and Gold Commissioner. So he remained in Rossland with his wife and their two sons.

In 1896, the output of the mines increased to the $1,000,000 mark. On February 1, the furnaces of Heinze's smelter at Trail Creek Landing were blown in and by fall, two rival railroads were racing to the Golden City. Heinze's narrow gauge of 14 tortuous miles of curves and switchbacks had been begun as the Trail Creek Tramway. However, a name change was instituted during construction and the line that reached the LeRoi mine in June was now called the Columbia & Western Railway (C&W). Six months later Corbin's crew drove home the last spike on the Red Mountain Railway. It's equally tortuous route of curves and spiral loops entered the city from the west via the Paterson Valley and Northport. The inducement for both companies was the increasing ore output from the Rossland mines.

By 1897, the mighty LeRoi was paying $25,000 a month in dividends. The directors, however, dissatisfied with the way the ore was being handled at the Trail smelter, decided to build their own smelting complex at Northport, and by that fall their

new smelter was completed and operating. Now Rossland had not only two railroads competing for its ore, but two smelters as well.

Incorporated as a city in March, 1897, Rossland had a population of 7,000 and was the third largest city in B.C. Big and brash, it boasted four breweries, more than 40 hotels and saloons of all descriptions, no less than two daily and three weekly newspapers, three banks, six churches and an opera house in its many establishments.

By 1898, Rossland was acclaimed as the premier camp of the province. But 1898 was to be a year of changes, some of which were to have a lasting effect on the future of the town. Heinze, with a looming legal battle against Standard Oil and Anaconda in Butte, Montana, sold out his entire Trail Creek interests to the CPR for just under $1,000,000. The CPR had only been interested in the charter of the C&W so it could counter the threat from the GNR into southern B.C. Heinze, however, insisted that his smelter be included in the deal. At first the CPR balked, threatening instead to construct a competing smelter at Blueberry Creek. But they eventually capitulated and appointed Walter Aldridge to secure a deal with Heinze.

*(Right) The first power plant at the LeRoi Mine is seen here during the course of construction.*

*(Opposite page) Another view of Rossland's Columbia Avenue.*

*(Below) Shipping ore from the LeRoi mine.*

Once the deal was completed, Heinze left the area to confront and eventually defeat his great opponents in the courtrooms of Montana.

This was the year, too, when Whittaker Wright's gigantic British America Corporation (BAC), after much bitter litigation with American minority shareholders, finally became undisputed owner of the LeRoi mine.

The sale, for $3,000,000, precipitated a lawsuit that lasted for a year and involved courts in Canada, United States and Britain. The controversy arose when a minority group of Spokane based shareholders, who had wanted to hold out for $5,000,000, initiated a lawsuit under U.S. law. The majority faction, with headquarters in Rossland, defended themselves under the rules of British law. Elsie Turnbull, in *Trail: A Smelter City* describes the situation:

"The minority group (headed by Turner) insisted that as the company was registered in the State of Washington it was not subject to British law and that since no alien cold hold property in Washington the BAC could not run the Northport smelter. Secretary Williams of the LeRoi Company feared that the Turner group might try to impound company documents so he gathered them together and took them from Spokane to Rossland, only to find he had been forestalled by the substitution of another seal in place of that belonging to the LeRoi Company. The BAC and the majority group were rendered powerless to transact any legal business."

The minority group then obtained an injunction prohibiting members of the majority group from leaving the United States. To enforce the order, deputies were hired to stop all trains leaving Spokane for Canada. Charles Mackintosh, of the BAC, countered by hiring a special train to whisk away three important shareholders. When Mackintosh and his party boarded the train, however, they were met by Sheriff Bruce who tried to prevent their departure. Finally Austin Corbin, the rail-

road's president, ordered the train to leave. As it headed north, Bruce held a revolver on the crew and remained aboard until Northport was reached. Told he would be arrested in Canada for carrying a weapon, he finally disembarked.

Upon his arrival in Rossland, Mackintosh had the LeRoi placed in receivership and had W.J. Harris ousted as manager. The majority group accused Harris of gutting the mine by shipping as much ore as possible to Northport, away from Canadian jurisdiction. However, the receivership was set aside, Harris was re-instated as mine manager, and shipments were continued to Northport.

The Turner faction then applied for an injunction restraining the BAC from taking possession of LeRoi stock held in escrow in the Bank of British North America in Rossland. "Mackintosh countered by announcing that the BAC assigned all its rights to shares of the LeRoi Company to the Corporation's assignee who was represented by the Bank of Montreal in Rossland. J.S.C. Fraser, manager of the Bank of Montreal, then wrote to the manager of the Bank of British North America advising that he had been instructed to pay the Bank of B.N.A. the sum of $1,042,054 and take delivery of LeRoi shares. He enclosed a cheque signed by C.H. Mackintosh, and received the shares for BAC."

Finally, late in November, a settlement was reached at a compromise price. The remaining stock was handed over to the BAC who thus became sole owners of the LeRoi property. Spokane financiers withdrew from Rossland, no longer in control, but well rewarded for their efforts.

For the next two years the town stabilized and the mines increased their output of gold and copper to more than $3,000,000 per year.

The turn of the century came and went quietly, but in the next 10 years, a series of events occurred which were to excite the town. In 1901, an enduring strike at the mines slowed production. A year later, much of the business section of the city was gutted by the first of the great Rossland fires and in 1905, another catastrophe rocked the town when, early one December afternoon, the powder house at the Centre Star mine mysteriously exploded with such force that the detonation was heard more than 10 miles away. Miraculously, only one life was lost.

In that same year, an embryo company was launched when the Centre Star and War Eagle mines, the Trail Smelter, the great St. Eugene mine at Moyie and the Rossland Power Company merged under the name of the Canadian Consolidated Mines. Within a decade, after the acquisition of the incomparable Sullivan mine at Kimberley and the once unwilling LeRoi mine, this new company, by then known as the Consolidated Mining and Smelting Company of Canada (COMINCO), emerged as one of the mining giants of the nation.

Before and after consolidation, the Rossland mines continued to pour their wealth and between 1901 and 1916, 50 percent of the entire gold production of B.C. came from the depths of the prolific mines on Red Mountain.

By the end of World War I, however, the mines finally showed signs of ore depletion. By 1920 the GNR abandoned its once productive Red Mountain line and within a year had pulled up its steel. It was an indication of things to come as the ore output continued to decrease with each passing year. Finally, in 1929, COMINCO, failing to come up with any significant ore bodies and with values decreasing with depth, reluctantly closed their Rossland mines. It was that year that the last company miner left the historic mountain which, for more than three illustrous decades, had been one of the greatest El Dorados in the west.

In the same year, the town received yet another blow when the last great Rossland fire laid waste to many of the businesses lining Columbia Avenue. By 1930, with the depression gradually lengthening and tightening its grip, the population skidded to less than 1,500 and the city's fortunes hit a new low. It was openly predicted in some quarters that Rossland was doomed to become another ghost town like Phoenix, the once great mining camp of the Boundary country.

But some mining towns die hard and some don't die at all — Rossland was one of the latter and it hung on until 1932 when it received an unexpected reprieve — the price of gold was suddenly raised to $35 an ounce. COMINCO threw its properties on Red Mountain open for lease, and once unprofitable ground suddenly became interesting.

Once again the old mines resounded with activity as dozens, then scores, and finally hundreds of men began reworking old dumps, cleaning out stopes and looking for new leads. The Midnight, I.X.L., Snowdrop and other O.K. Mountain properties came across profitable pockets of ore. From the South Belt area the Hattie, Lily May, Mayflower and Bluebird resumed shipping and once prominent names came to the fore once more as the LeRoi, Centre Star and War Eagle led all the custom shippers from the region.

For five years the leasers worked the original mines and in 1934, at the height of the new era, the total output approached a respectable $1,000,000. The revival, however spectacular at times, was brief and it was the last gasp for the ore bodies were virtually exhausted. By the beginning of the Second World War, the mines lay idle once again.

During the war years, the salvagers removed most of the workings on the once famous hill. As the old familiar landmarks gradually disappeared, only ore dumps, tunnels and shafts remained to verify the mountain's once formidable reputation. Claims like the Iron Horse, Jumbo, Rainy Day and Little Darling have long been memories, and today the eagle high city has relinquished its title as "Mining Capital of the Kootenays."

But a walk down Columbia Avenue is still a walk with history. The elegant courthouse, unchanged since 1900, still presides over the avenue as it did then, and here and there other traces of the past remain; the Central Hotel, now called the Irvin, has kept much of its old atmosphere and the hotel known as the Allan stands on the same site it did nearly a century ago. In the older section of the town, turn of the century architecture is still evident and many of the street names like Butte, Spokane and Washington continue to reflect the once prominent American accent in the old town. Although the eerie whistle of the GNR can no longer be heard coming in from the west, and the ore trains of the C&W can no longer be seen inching up the tortuous South Belt grade, the mood has not vanished. The mind can still almost visualize the miners, jostling elbow to elbow, along once busy Columbia Avenue and nearly hear the sound of blasting at the mines once more — and the memories flood back, memories of other days — when the town was still known as The Golden City and the LeRoi was the king of Red Mountain.    ♣

# 6

# THE KASLO & SLOCAN RAILWAY

*Constructed in 1895 for $750,000, the Kaslo & Slocan Railway was an event of great importance to Kaslo and the Silvery Slocan. Its construction accelerated the recovery from the depression of 1893 and was a tremendous boost for local business.*

T HE first mineral claim in the Silvery Slocan was staked on Payne Mountain on September 9, 1891. Before the year was out 191 claims, most of them in the snow, had been recorded. During 1892 an additional 633 claims were recorded. As the richness of these mines became apparent, it was realized that some means of transporting the ore to market was crucial.

A railway from Bonner's Ferry, Idaho, to the foot of Kootenay Lake was under construction in the early 1890s, and in conjunction with this rail service, a line of steamboats was inaugurated on the lake. The boat service was known as the International Navigation and Trading Company, and its primary objective was to call at the various ports on the lake and funnel traffic out of the Kootenays into the waiting arms of the Great Northern Railway (GNR). One of the ports served was Kaslo, the outlet for the ore from the mines in the Sandon district. Initially, ore from the Slocan mines was shipped to Kaslo by mules and horses over a rough trail. As this trail was improved into a road, wagons were used to haul the ore. However, it was soon realized that for better transport a railway had to be built.

Two companies applied to the provincial government for a charter to build a railway from Kaslo to Sandon. One group was headed by D.C. Corbin, whose Nelson & Fort Sheppard Railway (N&FS) was already under construction from the United States border to Nelson. The other applicants were Alex Ewen, D.J. Munn and John Hendry of New Westminster. They proposed to build a broad gauge line known as the Kaslo & Slocan Railway (K&S). On April 23, 1892, Ewen, Munn and Hendry were awarded the charter. The agreement included a land grant of 10,240 acres of land, for each mile of railway, and freedom from taxes for 10 years.

With this inducement, the work of building the railway was expected to begin promptly. But, except for a preliminary survey, which was completed in December, nothing further was done that year. Then, in April, 1893, the Nelson *Miner* reported that Corbin had offered to purchase the K&S charter from Ewen, Munn and Hendry for $100,000. This offer was rejected, however, the K&S owners demanding $200,000. Corbin considered this price a trifle high, and refused.

In July, unconfirmed rumours began to circulate that James J. Hill, owner of the GNR, had purchased the K&S. Three months later, one of Hill's engineers was in

*(Above) A construction crew on the Kaslo & Slocan line just outside Kaslo.*
*(Below) The wood burning No. 2 locomotive of the Kaslo & Slocan Railway.*

Kaslo carefully looking over the ground. This fuelled speculation that if Hill had not already purchased the K&S, he was about to do so. By the end of November some 80 men were employed clearing the right of way and work was reported to be "proceeding steadily."

But the K&S was apparently unable to obtain financial backing for their project, and in April, 1894, K&S officials were in Victoria trying to get funding from the government. When their efforts appeared to be failing, they telegraphed Kaslo to send a 20-man delegation to plead their case. One of the delegates, G.O. Buchanan, was quoted in the Victoria *Times* as saying: "The railway company on whom the people of Kaslo had depended to assist them on developing the mines had been unable to finance their scheme on account of the government aid given to the Nakusp & Slocan railway. Financiers would not help a railway company in opposition with a road that had been furthered and would probably be maintained by the government. The delegation asked as a matter of justice that the people of Kaslo and Kootenay Lake be placed on the same footing as the people on the other side of the same district, as far as government aid to railways was concerned."

Following the meeting there was a rumour that Kaslo had received a message stating the government had agreed with every request made by the K&S, including a guarantee of interest at four percent on company bonds to the extent of $10,000 per mile. A week later the *Miner* defused this rumour by stating the K&S had to content "themselves with little better than nothing, not even securing such terms as the Chilliwack or Nicola Valley railways." However, the railway had been successful in having their charter amended from a broad gauge to narrow. They also had the land grant altered so that the company could select 60,000 acres of land located elsewhere in B.C.

Despite the lack of financial support from the government, K&S officials promised that the railway would be completed at once. But it was not until March, 1895, that the contract was awarded to Foley Brothers & Guthrie of St. Paul, Minnesota. Two more months passed before the Three Forks *Slocan Prospector* was able to list the sub-contractors. James McDonell, a Montana railway builder, got the first three miles from Kaslo, "and already has about 100 men shovelling dirt. Jim Walsh, the Italian has the next three miles." Pat Walsh was awarded the next three miles, followed by Cameron & Porter with six miles, McLean, McBeth & McLean with nine miles and J.W. Stewart with three miles. All told there were about a dozen camps along the line and it was estimated 700 to 1,000 men would be employed.

In July Supt. Charles Folliot advised the *Slocan Prospector* that more than half of the 30 miles was rapidly taking shape. He expressed confidence that the first nine miles leading out of Kaslo would be completed in 30 days, "and there is none of the grading on the line that will not be finished in 60 days. Steel rails for the road will begin to arrive in Kaslo by the 20th of the present month, and soon thereafter a construction train will be put on and the road completed within the time specified at the commencement of building."

At Kaslo meanwhile, Porter Brothers had already commenced construction on a 24-foot-wide, 1,000-foot-long wharf that was needed immediately to receive the rails and rolling stock. Two weeks later the *Slocan Prospector* advised its readers that plans for over 30 bridges, the largest to be 420 feet long, were being drawn up in the Kaslo office. Three other bridges were also worthy of note: a 60-foot span across Kaslo Creek above 15 Mile House; an 80-foot span at Payne Bluff; and a

140-foot span across Carpenter Creek between Sandon and Cody.

Owing to the difficult mountainous terrain, it was not until October 23, 1895, that the line finally reached Sandon. Reported the Kaslo *Claim:* "At 3:30 Wednesday afternoon the K&S rails were laid into Sandon amidst great rejoicing by the people, who celebrated the event with a ball and a big time generally.

"Before Wednesday of next week Supt. McGraw informs the *Claim* the tracks will be at Cody, the end of the line, and November 15 will witness the completion of the road in every detail." Regular service was inaugurated on November 20, and in the first full year of operation the railway ran 32,674 train miles, transported 28,307 passengers and 23,734 tons of freight — and made a tidy profit of slightly more than $66,000.

Compared with our two great rail systems or even the Pacific Great Eastern (BC Rail), the K&S was just a small railroad. Its tightly curved and heavily graded three-foot gauge mainline was only 28.8 miles long, but in the last decade of the 19th century it was very important. Built to transport ore containing lead, zinc and silver from the mines in the Sandon district, to Kaslo on the way to smelters in the United States, it formed a part of one of many thrusts of the GNR to tap business in southern British Columbia.

The line throughout was laid with steel rails that weighed 45 pounds per yard. With a total trackage of 33.4 miles that included a three-mile spur from Sandon to Cody, the roadbed was rough, winding and steep. From the terminus at Kaslo, the line gained altitude quickly by means of a switchback, then followed the Kaslo River past Fish and Bear lakes, climbing up the side of the mountain until it reached the site of Zincton. Old-timers claim that if the stumps got too large, the K&S line ran around them. From there the going was really tough, and Payne Bluff, with its sheer drop of 1,080 feet, was rounded on a rocky ledge, with a "grasshopper" trestle, just before reaching Three Forks. Nervous passengers were warned not to look out the window at this point. The line ran into Sandon about four miles further on and bent right around the town, coming in on the east and finishing up on the west. The Cody extension left the mainline some distance below Sandon and, rising rapidly, passed 300 feet above the mainline.

To operate the railway, the K&S purchased second-hand equipment. Baldwin locomotives, numbers 1 and 2 with a 2-6-0 wheel arrangement were bought from the Alberta Railway and Coal Company. Early rolling stock was two wooden coaches and 20 freight cars. Later, the GNR provided locomotive number 3, a 2-8-0 for freight service, and the number of freight cars was increased to 47. The increase of passenger traffic also necessitated the addition of two more passenger cars.

Prior to the K&S being built, the Canadian Pacific Railway (CPR) had constructed a branch line from Nakusp, on Slocan Lake, with its terminus at Three Forks. This line, called the Nakusp and Slocan Railway (N&S), had one major drawback. Ore had to be hauled down to the railhead in wagons from Sandon, which was four miles up the valley. The K&S, however, had built right into Sandon, giving it a distinct advantage. Not to be outdone, the N&S decided to push into Sandon as well. This extension was very much disliked by the K&S, and for some time feelings ran very high in that wild mining community. These bitter feelings came to a boil just before Christmas in 1895.

The problem began some time earlier when the N&S, without first obtaining permission, or even consulting the K&S, built a new depot and laid tracks upon

*(Above) Alex Ewen, left, and John Hendry, centre, together with D.J. Munn, not shown, received a charter to construct the Kaslo & Slocan Railway. They had originally proposed to build a broad gauge line, but it was later revised to a narrow gauge.*

*(Above right) Richard Marpole, General Manager for the CPR, came to Sandon to witness the destruction of the N&S's new depot by the K&S.*

*(Left) James J. Hill. He eventually took control of the Kaslo & Slocan Railway. Later, when the railway was facing hard times, he tried unsuccessfully to negotiate a deal with his old foe, the CPR.*

*(Opposite page) This painting by B.C. artist Bill Maximick, depicts the Kaslo & Slocan rounding Payne Bluff near Sandon.*

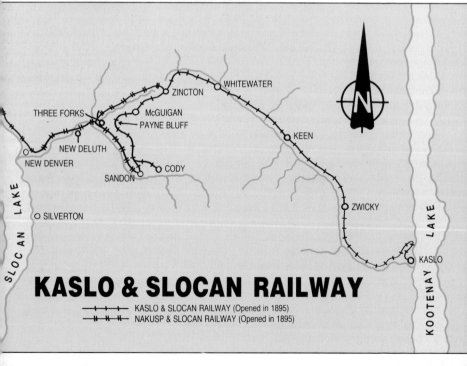

# KASLO & SLOCAN RAILWAY

—+—+—+— KASLO & SLOCAN RAILWAY (Opened in 1895)
—H—H—H— NAKUSP & SLOCAN RAILWAY (Opened in 1895)

grounds claimed by the K&S. The K&S first obtained a court injunction against the N&S, then proceeded to move by force the objectionable material. However, after a few days the CPR had the injunction set aside and at once began to rebuild. They laid their tracks and constructed a fine depot building. All was quiet for a time and it appeared that the K&S had knuckled under to the N&S. But the K&S was merely trying to determine where it stood legally.

Finally, on Sunday, December 15, having received instructions from Victoria, the K&S moved into action. At about 8 p.m. some 60 or 70 able-bodied men assembled at the Kaslo station armed with tools of every description. It was assumed by observers that they were going to repair a large bridge somewhere on the line, but that presumption was soon to be proved false.

Under the leadership of Manager Charles Folliot and Superintendent McGraw, the men reached Sandon about 3 a.m. Monday morning. When they arrived they found Mr. Clements, the contractor putting up the buildings for the N&S, Mr. Hamilton, the agent and telegraph operator, and a few other men asleep in the boarding car, which was placed on the track at point (B) on the accompanying sketch. At point (A) stood a freight car waiting to be loaded with ore from the Reco mine.

The K&S people began their operation by turning the switch at point (C) and starting the cars in motion. The freight car, going first, jumped the track at the switch, the boarding car bumping into it pretty roughly. By the time the boarding car started rolling most of the occupants were awake, and as its momentum increased, Clements jumped and landed on some boards, getting severely bruised. The others stayed with the car until the collision, when the stove pinned the agent to the wall, making a large bruise to his leg. Fortunately the stove was cold. The other men in the car were badly shaken, but not seriously hurt.

The work of destruction was now begun. The freight shed was quickly torn down and the remains thrown upon lands the K&S did not claim. The bridge (D) forming the new road put in by the N&S was demolished and the posts sawed off. The platform (E), which blocked the way of the old government wagon road, was destroyed. The ties and rails to point (F) were torn up and also part of the platform, rails and ties to point (G). Satisfied with their morning's work, the K&S people then went to breakfast.

Mr. Lawrence, roadmaster for the N&S, and Mr. Johnson soon arrived on the scene and, after surveying the damage, attempted to re-lay the track. However, Folliot had lined his men up at point (F), and when the N&S men attempted to put a tie down, it was immediately ripped up and thrown after them. The N&S men then attempted to enter the disputed ground but were forcibly moved back by the K&S. When Clement's employees entered the station to commence work, they were immediately stopped and escorted out again. The station, 50x22 feet, and partly two stories, was the only building left standing on the disputed ground.

Coded telegrams were quickly sent to N&S officials, and an attempt was made to obtain a warrant for the arrest of Superintendent McGraw. However, Judge Sproat refused to issue the warrant, saying he thought the K&S were right. Rumours then began circulating in the Sandon saloons that Supt. Richard Marpole was on his way from the CPR mainline with 400 men and would arrive in Sandon at 9 a.m. Tuesday morning. Meanwhile, the remainder of Monday passed quietly.

Shortly after 12 noon on Tuesday, a K&S train arrived and a crowd of men

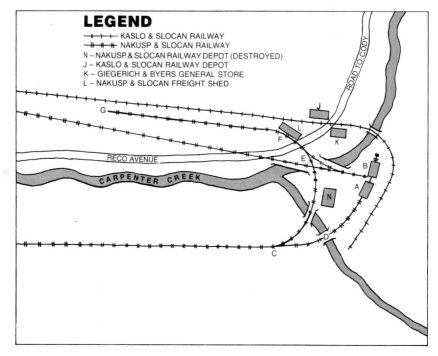

swarmed out and immediately began to attack the N&S station with axes and hammers. Remonstrations by N&S officials against the destruction of the depot went unheeded, and as they watched helplessly, a cable was wrapped around the building and fastened to the K&S engine. Then, amidst the yells of the crowd, the train moved slowly forward. A few minutes later the N&S's new depot was nothing but a mass of jumbled lumber.

A few minutes later the N&S train carrying Marpole, McGillivery, Lawrence, Johnson and a few others pulled into Sandon. Expecting trouble, Superintendent McGraw ordered his men to form a line and throw anyone back who attempted to cross, but no attempt was made. After quietly looking over the ground, and issuing instructions for the rearrangements of the tracks, Marpole left Sandon about 3:30 p.m. A short time later the K&S train pulled out with its officials for Kaslo, "leaving all quiet at the seat of war."

Marpole refused to discuss the incident with a reporter from the Nelson *Miner,* but Folliot was only to happy to do so. He said he regretted the destruction of property which had taken place, but laid the blame solely on the CPR. He claimed that he had been forced to demolish the new depot because CPR officials refused to stay off the disputed ground until the matter could be resolved in court. "Had the N&S people agreed, when asked on Monday to give an undertaking not to trespass, until the matter could be decided in the courts, the pulling down (of) the station building of the N&S could have been avoided, but he could get no promise and his instructions had to be carried out."

Thus ended the railway war between the K&S and the N&S. Remarkably, it had ended without anyone being seriously injured. The CPR, apparently recognizing

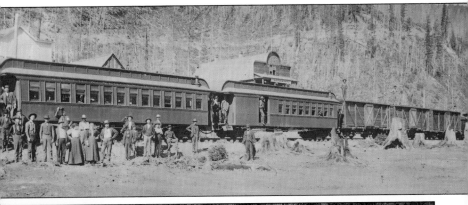

(Top) The Kaslo & Slocan Railway train at Whitewater.
(Above) The remains of Whitewater, also known as Retallack, today.
(Opposite page) The town of Zincton before the buildings were set afire and destroyed.
(Below) The remains of the Kaslo & Slocan Railway trestle at Whitewater in 1989.

the K&S's claim to the disputed ground, although belatedly, did not pursue the matter further.

But while this incident may have been forgotten, the intense rivalry between the two lines continued, and on August 21, 1897, the Sandon *Mining Review* reported that the CPR planned to extend the N&S from Three Forks to Whitewater. "The proposed extension will seriously cripple the business of the K&S, as it will be a competitor for the large volume of business at McGuigan and Whitewater." There were between 25 and 30 shipping points that would be affected, and the *Mining Review* speculated that the K&S would retaliate by extending their railway to Slocan Lake. This could have been done at relatively little cost, and, in fact, a survey party had already located a route from Bear Lake to Three Forks. "There is good reason to believe that the party will continue in the field until a survey is made to Silverton," claimed the paper. However, neither extension was built.

On January 1, 1899, the K&S, together with the steamboat line on Kootenay Lake and the GNR line (Bonners Ferry to the foot of the lake) were taken over by a company incorporated in London, England under the name Kootenay Railway and Navigation Company. While this was a British firm, the GNR retained its controlling interest. The K&S may be said to have started its downward direction from this time. Although the revenue from the transportation of zinc alone amounted to almost $90,000 in one year, the GNR allowed the line to deteriorate until it finally abandoned it altogether.

In 1900 a disastrous fire wiped out most of Sandon and, although the town was rebuilt to some extent, it was never the same again. From then on deficits appeared and while the mining business was still good, the railway dropped into the red. The line was very difficult to maintain, there were many company structures which were continually damaged by the ravages of nature in the form of snowslides and landslides, fire and storms. The cost of maintenance bit heavily into what might have been a profit and snow removal added greatly to the expenses.

"The establishment of lead smelting in Canada had deprived the Company of its long haul to smelters in the United States," wrote Margery Ringheim in *Historical Kaslo.* "Thereafter, no interest was taken in the line. They failed to provide adequate facilities, mining operators paid exorbitant prices, and met with endless delays. The ore came down from the mines to Kaslo in box cars and gondolas, where it was wheel-barrowed onto scows towed by another company to Troupe Junction, then wheel-barrowed again to standard gauge cars. This primitive method was exceedingly costly, and the cost was born by the shippers. Even the G.N. lake steamers were pictures of ruin and neglect. The *Alberta* was being used as a houseboat. The *Kaslo,* badly battered and roughly boarded up, was rotting on the ways at Mirror Lake. The *Argenta* was high and dry on the beach at Kaslo, while the *International* was the only one afloat. However, its smokestack was half-mast and its boiler missing."

By mid-June, 1901, there were rumours floating about that James Hill and Thomas Shaughnesy had come to an arrangement for a division of B.C. territory by which the CPR would take over the K&S. But, although CPR officials were negotiating with Hill, the deal fell through and the K&S was left on its own to survive as best it could.

Four months later a day coach left the track at Sandon and was demolished. The accident happened on the Cody spur on Thursday afternoon, October 17. While the K&S train crew was doing some switching at the Reco siding, they left the day coach standing on the main track with the brakes set. The *Sandon Paystreak* describes what happened next: "When the air relaxed it left all the pressure on the hand brake and the coach started down the grade. The trainmen saw the coach start but were unable to catch it. There were only two passengers aboard, Mrs. Winter and child of Cody. Gaining momentum as it went the coach shot down past Sandon at a terrific speed. Near the foot of the steep grade there is a sudden turn in the little track, and here the coach jumped the rails and piled up against the rock cut, breaking the woodwork of the car finer than toothpicks. By what seems almost a miracle Mrs. Winter and her child escaped instant death. When rescuers arrived they were taken from the wreck to their home in Cody where they are under medical care."

Despite accidents and decreasing revenue, it was the forces of nature that ultimately sealed the fate of the K&S. During 1908, numerous landslides caused extensive damage to the track. In 1909 further landslides took out bridges and track to such an extent that the line from McGuigan to Sandon was abandoned. An abbreviated service was kept up between Kaslo and McGuigan until 1910. Then, in July, the final crushing blow came in a tremendous forest fire which practically wiped out all stations, buildings and most of the remaining bridges, twisting the rails so badly that operations ceased altogether. A "sort of train" made a weekly trip up the remaining 14 miles of track, but no effort was made toward repairing or restoring the damaged line. Then, on December 24, an ominous notice was posted: "Account of illness of engineer, impossible to operate train on the K&S until further notice. Public will be advised re trains later. P.H. Walsh, Supt."

That was virtually the end of the K&S as a narrow gauge line and was a serious setback for the community of Kaslo. The Kaslo Board of Trade responded by firing a telegram off to the head officials in St. Paul. They were ignored until a second telegram was sent demanding an answer. But the reply, stating ". . .the matter was under consideration," was not very encouraging.

When several weeks passed without further word, the Board of Trade appealed to Premier McBride that the GNR be forced to make its intentions known. The Premier responded immediately and was advised by GNR officials that the line would be repaired and reopened to Sandon. However, after a few meagre repairs, the work was again abandoned. A resolution was then sent to the Legislature arguing that the GNR had received a land grant of 212,763 acres and had been exempted from taxation for several years, and unless they were prepared to live up to the terms of their charter, it should be cancelled. But not even the threatened cancellation of the charter made any difference. The GNR had lost interest and nothing would persuade them to invest money to repair the line.

In January, 1911, the matter was placed before the provincial cabinet in Victoria and Premier McBride eventually obtained satisfaction from GNR officials on April 21, 1911, when word was received that they had finally agreed to dispose of the K&S right of way and rolling stock for $25,000.

Previous efforts to interest the CPR in the K&S had proved futile and it now became apparent that a local syndicate would have to be formed to take up the option. "A public meeting was called and $19,000 was guaranteed before it opened," wrote Ringheim. "A second $25,000 had to be raised for operating expenses, but liberal aid was received from the government which proposed to guarantee the bonds of a new company to the extent of $200,000 free of interest for three years,

*(Above) This train, headed by locomotive #2 of the K&S, is westbound at mile 15.85 from Kaslo, in the Kaslo River Canyon.*
*(Opposite page) The abandoned roadbed of the K&S at Zincton in 1986. (Top inset) Remains of the old water tower at Zincton. (Bottom inset) The remains of the town of Zincton in 1986, after the buildings were set afire and destroyed.*

then with 4 per cent interest. Also, the government was to take over the road-bed and reimburse the owners to the extent of the purchase price if, at the end of three years, the company found they could not operate the line to advantage."

Plans were made for reconstructing the line and bridges to a standard gauge. New motive power and steel cars were to be purchased, and the line was to be put in shape to McGuigan as soon as possible. Later, if conditions warranted it, an extension would be made to Sandon. The members of the local syndicate greeted these plans enthusiastically, and the future of the K&S looked brighter than it had for many months. But news that the CPR were extending the N&S six miles from Three Forks to near Zincton, soon dampened their enthusiasm. The construction of such a spur would mean that ore from the Whitewater and Lucky Jim would be sent over the N&S and make it virtually impossible for the K&S to operate successfully.

"H. Giegerich and James Anderson were sent by City Council to interview Sir Thomas Shaughnessy at Montreal and point out to him that the building of this spur would ruin the K&S Railway Company and cause the mines from Bear Lake to Kaslo to be without transportation facilities other than the old wagon road — (a road which had been repaired but was of little use to the mine operators in comparison with the railway)." Sir Thomas was courteous, but CPR officials felt it was in the best interest of the CPR to build the spur. Eventually the K&S syndicate repaired 15 miles of line and operated a service with a gasoline track car. But it proved to be too expensive.

Eventually, in February, 1912, as a result of government negotiations, the CPR agreed to take over the line. An agreement was drawn into whereby the CPR was to maintain and operate the railway as part of its system in B.C. A grant of $100,000 was made by the government and as a result the CPR started work on the line. It was standard gauge and most of the original right of way was used. The CPR already had its line from Zincton around to Sandon, so it was not necessary to repair the old line around Payne Bluff. The two tracks were connected at Zincton with the whole being known as the Kaslo Subdivision. It is interesting to note that this subdivision did not have actual rail connection to the mainline, all traffic came to it by car ferry on Slocan Lake.

The affairs of the local syndicate were wound up with the sale of equipment, the narrow gauge locos going to logging concerns on the Pacific coast, where it was presumed they worked until the narrow gauge was finally banned for logging operations. All subscriptions were refunded and a dividend of 10 per cent declared. The new railway was opened on July 1, 1914 with a free excursion trip from Kaslo to Nakusp. The CPR continued to operate the K&S until 1955 when torrential rains washed out several hundred yards of track at Three Forks. For several years before this the line had only been used to transport freight, so it was considered impractical to rebuild it.

Even if the ravages of nature had not taken place, it is extremely doubtful if the K&S would have survived until today as a narrow gauge railway. Changing times and economics sealed the doom of most short lines and the K&S, located in a rugged, sparsely populated territory would have felt the blow early. One by one the few remaining vestiges of the K&S are disappearing. A few years ago the monumental wooden viaduct, a short distance west of Zincton, which could be seen from the CPR line across the creek, and which had been standing as a mute reminder of the roaring narrow gauge days, disappeared in a matter of seconds when struck by an avalanche.

It is claimed by some old-timers that some of the rusting rails are still in place on the mountain ledges near Payne Bluff. Even after 60 years some of the spots served by the K&S remain inaccessible. One thing is certain, the mountains and valleys will never again echo to the exhaust and the whistles of the little narrow gauge Moguls battling the grades between Kaslo and Sandon, and it is no consolation that it was not the diesel that put them out of business.　　　　　♣

# 7
# GHOST TOWNS
# OF THE SILVERY SLOCAN

*Today, the Silvery Slocan is quiet, serene, and practically deserted.*
*But in the mid-1890s through the early 1900s, the area enjoyed*
*unprecedented growth as thousands swarmed in. The attraction*
*was the rich silver-lead ore from which the region derived its nickname.*

T HE first man known to have searched for minerals in the Slocan was Robert
Baird. In 1884, Baird, accompanied by an Indian, prospected the creeks of
the Slocan searching for placer gold. In one of the creeks near the future
town-site of Three Forks he found colours, but not in paying quantities. Discouraged,
Baird left the region and made his way to East Kootenay where he gained employment with Eddy, Hammond & Co. That November, while transporting the company's
receipts to Montana, he was bushwhacked and murdered by Bull Dog Kelly 24 miles
south of Golden.

Two years later Capt. George Sanderson, Jack Evans and a German made their
way into the Slocan by way of the as yet unnamed Carpenter Creek. Like Baird,
they too were searching for placer or lode gold; and like Baird, they also made
their way inland as far as the future town-site of Three Forks. Plenty of galena was
found, but it was considered worthless at the time and ignored, and this party also
left the area.

It was not until the summer of 1891 that the richness of Slocan's treasure vault
would begin to surface. It began when three prospectors, Andrew Jardine, John
Allen and Jack McDonald, found a promising outcrop of silver in the Blue Ridge
Mountains about 13 miles up Kaslo Creek and staked the Beaver claim. In August,
Jardine returned to Ainsworth with a quantity of high grade silver-lead ore. Prompted
by this discovery, a number of prospectors decided to investigate the area. Among
them were Eli Carpenter and John L. Seaton, and it was their discovery that put
the Silvery Slocan on the map.

Born in Knoxville, Tennessee, in 1858, Seaton left home at a young age and went
to Colorado, where he worked in the mines for several years. From Colorado,
Seaton went to Montana, and from there to the Coeur d'Alenes. In 1889, Seaton
arrived in Ainsworth, and for a time was employed in the Skyline mine as a timber-
man.

Carpenter was born in Paris, France, around 1843. He later travelled to New York
where he joined P.T. Barnum's circus as a tightrope walker. In the 1880s, Carpenter
decided to forego his circus background and seek his fortune in mining. Leaving
his wife to live with her sister in New Hampshire, Carpenter arrived at Wild Horse

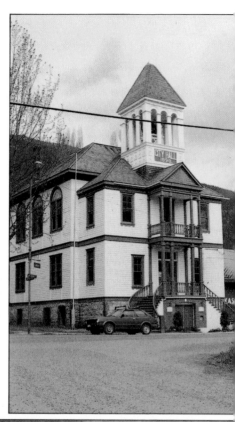

(Above) "Lardo" Jack McDonald and Andrew Jardine at their Beaver claim in
1891. It was this discovery that interested
other prospectors to the area.
(Right) The Kaslo City Hall was built in
1898. Today it is used as a library.
(Below) A general view of Kaslo in 1897.

*(Right) St. Andrew's United Church. Built in 1893 entirely of volunteer labour, it was Kaslo's first church and is the oldest church in B.C. continuously in use. It is shown in the photo below on the far right. (Below) The Langham Cultural Centre began its career as a hotel (it is shown as white building in photo directly below). It was later occupied by a bank and a bottling company, and during WWII was used as internment housing for Japanese-Canadians exiled from the coast. By the mid-1970s, the Langham was derelict, but rather than tear it down, the people of Kaslo rebuilt it.*

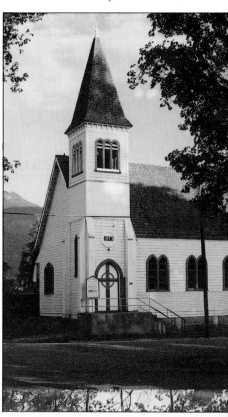

Creek in B.C. in 1884 or 1885 and established a placer claim. Each year for the next six years, he sent his wife $2,000 in gold. Carpenter and his French-Canadian wife had been deeply in love, but the long separation must have proven too lonely for her. One day a letter arrived from her sister advising Carpenter that his wife was about to become a mother. Since the baby was obviously not his, Carpenter was deeply hurt by the news. Immediately he abandoned the Wild Horse diggings and made his way to West Kootenay, soon finding himself in Ainsworth. When news of the Beaver claim reached that town, Carpenter and Seaton formed a partnership and set out to find their fortunes.

By early September, Seaton and Carpenter had penetrated further westward than the other prospectors and found themselves within sight of Slocan Lake. Their search to this point had been unsuccessful, and the two men decided to return to Ainsworth. However, when a dispute arose over which route to take, the two men decided to divided their outfits. Seaton then headed east while Carpenter started out for Slocan Lake.

According to the February 4, 1894 issue of the Nelson *Tribune:* "In retracing his steps, Seaton discovered the outcroppings of the Payne mine. While engaged in staking the claim he was overtaken by Carpenter, who had changed his mind regarding the route out." The date was September 9, 1891, and the Payne was the first location to be made in the soon to be famous Silvery Slocan. Seaton and Carpenter then hurried back to Ainsworth to have their specimens assayed.

At this point some historians claim Carpenter switched samples on Seaton and told his partner the ore was worthless. The Nelson *Miner,* the only newspaper published in West Kootenay at the time, does not collaborate such a claim. However, the issue of September 26, 1891, does seem to suggest that Carpenter tried to get back into the area without Seaton's knowledge. "On Monday last Eli Carpenter and E.A. Bielenberg of Ainsworth quietly packed up their blankets and left for the Slocan River, by way of Nelson."

Seaton is said to have been advised of this betrayal by a saloon keeper. Angered, he gathered together some friends for a prospecting party of his own. To again quote the *Miner:* "On Monday night about eight boats and probably 20 miners slipped away under the guidance of Jack Seaton and took the opposite route via Kaslo Creek."

The September 3, 1896 issue of the Nakusp *Ledge* published Carpenter's version of the events. "Eli says that when they reached Ainsworth, Jack swore he would never return, and he determined to return alone. He procured a supply of provisions at Nelson, and went in by way of Slocan Lake. When he arrived he found Jack Seaton and another party had got in two days in advance of him and staked the Noble Five and other claims, 26 in all. The old man was sore, but he could do nothing."

Ironically, neither Seaton nor Carpenter profited greatly from their discovery. Except for his part in the initial Payne discovery, Carpenter played no role in the future of the Slocan. In the fall of 1892 he was trying his luck in the Lardeau district. Unsuccessful there, he returned to the Slocan. On May 24, 1897, he astounded everyone in the region when he performed a high-wire act during celebrations at Slocan City. Spectators, unaware of his circus background, applauded loudly as he walked forward and backward across a wire strung from a third floor window. They stared in stunned silence, however, when he repeated the feat blindfolded and then cooked bacon and eggs on a stove halfway across. Alas, for Carpenter, it was a final hurrah. In September a local paper noted that he had left for the Klondike goldfields, where he reportedly died a year later. His total profit from the Payne discovery, depending on which source is correct, was either $500 or $1,000.

Seaton's fate was similarly tragic. Like Carpenter, Seaton sold his interest in the Payne to S.S. Bailey. He also sold several of his other interests and had little involvement in the Noble Five. In the spring of 1893 a younger brother came out from Tennessee, but died within two months. Seaton took his brother's body back to Tennessee for burial then, being a sick man himself, went to Hot Springs, Arkansas to recuperate. He remained there for six weeks, then returned to Spokane. A short time later he became ill and was bed-ridden. Death followed 10 days later.

The true sequence of events concerning the discovery of the Payne will never be precisely ascertained. What is known, however, is that by travelling the shorter, more direct route, the Seaton party reached the scene first. There, on October 5, 1891, Seaton, Jack and Bill Hennessey, Frank Flint and Jack McGuigan staked a group of claims, the riches of which turned out to be the Noble Five. Three days later an old prospector named John Sandon staked the Slocan Star. Sandon was in a party consisting of himself, Bruce White and Charles Chambers that located seven claims. Sandon later sold his interests to his partners. Two years later, Sandon drowned in the small creek which now bears his name.

Before the year ended, 191 claims, many of them in the snow, had been staked. By this time Ainsworth had been virtually deserted. Almost its entire population had rushed to the mouth of Kaslo Creek where George Kane, anticipating a rush two years earlier, had had the foresight to preempt a town-site. George sent for his younger brother David who, upon arrival, erected a log cabin. This was the first building to be erected on what was for a time known as Kane's Landing. David lived there alone during the summer or 1890, with only a small dog and a tame bear for company.

Following the discovery of the Payne, hundreds of people rushed to Kane's Landing, and almost overnight the new town, renamed Kaslo, had a transient population of about 600. Most of the earliest arrivals were prospectors who pitched tents in anticipation of a brief stay before continuing to the scene of mining activity. Others, however, decided to put up permanent establishments to cater to the needs of miners. By the spring of 1892, J.B. Wilson and Green Bros., the latter being a general merchant in Ainsworth, had established branch stores. Hotels, restaurants, saloons and other business establishments soon followed, and by summer Kaslo was a beehive of activity. Its main streets, lined with stores, were filled with miners and promoters. At night, the crowded bars of saloons and hotels like the Silver King, Grand Central, Slocan, Leland, Ottawa, Palace and Dardanelles resounded to blackjack and poker.

When it was realized that the centre of mining activity, which was 30 miles inland from Kaslo, was only five miles from the shores of Slocan Lake, many miners from Nelson chose the latter route. Within a month after the first discoveries had been made, the businessmen of Nelson had commenced a trail from the Columbia & Kootenay Railway up Slocan River. A month later 25 miles of the trail had been completed to a point where boats could be laden and rowed to the mouth of Carpenter Creek without difficulty.

Commenting on the stampede, the *Miner* wrote: ". . .half a hundred hardy, adven-

(Above) An early view of New Denver, first known as Eldorado.
(Opposite page) A view of Slocan Lake. Following the discovery by Seaton and Carpenter, prospectors soon realised that access to the area was easier by travelling up Slocan River and Lake to New Denver. From there, the centre of activity was only five miles away. (Top inset) Jonathan M. Harris. The man who's name is almost synonymous with Sandon, nearly drowned in Slocan Lake when his canoe overturned. (Bottom inset) The first log cabin in Kaslo. The central figure is David Kane. Note the pet bear on the roof.
(Bottom) An aerial view of New Denver in 1966.

turous prospectors will put in the winter in Slocan district. Bill Hunter and Billy McKinnon are already there; E.A. Bielenberg and his partners are in with supplies; Jack Evans, Jack Buchanan, Mike Landrigan and Bill Simcocks are on the way there; a party of Wisconsin men are half way up Slocan river with a ton of supplies; Jap King, George Long, and Ben Anderson started this week; C.M. Gething, W.R. Will, and S. Anderson made a break on Friday; Martin Fry started the same day; Bob Kirkwood left today; other parties whose names are not obtainable are either in or on their way in."

As more and more prospectors began to land on the flat at the mouth of Carpenter Creek, a small town, at first called Eldorado, began to take shape. In mid-January, 1892, the future New Denver had only a general store, operated by Hunter & Co., and four cabins. But in February, prospectors, miners and capitalists began heading up the Slocan in droves, and by the first week of April fully 500 men were camped in the neighbourhood of Eldorado and some 50 buildings had been erected. Two months later a trail had been completed from the new town clear through to Cody Creek, in the very heart of silver country. Approximately halfway along this trail, at the point where Carpenter, Seaton and Kane creeks converged, it was joined by the trail from Kaslo.

Along with the hundreds of prospectors who swarmed into the area in the spring of 1892 was a tireless individual named Jonathan Morgan Harris. Born in Vernon Mills, Virginia, in 1864, young Harris spent his childhood in the tobacco fields of Virginia before deciding to try his luck in Idaho's Coeur d'Alenes region. While there he heard the news of rich silver strikes in the Slocan and, greatly interested, he set off to seek his fortune.

After obtaining supplies in Nelson, Harris and a partner continued to the Slocan. At one point just before reaching Eldorado, their canoe was swamped in a storm and both men nearly drowned. Despite losing most of their gear, however, they pressed on and were soon at the centre of activity. In May, Harris located the Loudoun claim in a slight widening of Carpenter Creek near its junction with Sandon Creek. Harris was working this claim when, on July 5, a prospectors named Brown, from Nelson, located a promising claim on the nearby hillside.

Brown had only been in the area for two days when he happened to strike across a gulch in the neighbourhood of the Noble Five group. The area had been walked over by hundreds of prospectors and the ground all around had been staked off in the snow. But, by his fortuitous timing, Brown passed over the ground just after the snow melted and discovered eight feet of solid galena cropping right out of the earth. According to the July 23, 1892 issue of the Nelson *Miner,* Brown named his claim the Ruccan.

Harris, envisioning it as being better than his own, offered to purchase it for $2,700. A deal was struck and Harris settled the bargain by handing over a silver dollar, the only money he possessed at the time. Harris then formed a partnership with S.M. Wharton, F.T. Kelly and Evan Jones and renamed the mine the Reco. To obtain operating capital, they then issued $1,000,000 in shares, selling $100,000 worth and retaining the balance for themselves.

During that summer the woods were full of prospectors as mines like the Slocan Star, Freddie Lee, Noble Five, Payne, Reco and Wonderful began to produce. The ore was taken to Kaslo by George W. Hughes' pack mules, the principal freighter at the time, over a rough trail. At this time, the nearest town was New Denver, but that was all about to change.

# THREE FORKS AND NEW DULUTH

On June 14, 1892, Charles Hugonin and Erie C. Carpenter applied for a grant of land and obtained a preemption for a town-site at the junction of Carpenter, Seaton and Kane creeks, which they appropriately named Three Forks. Prior to this, George Hughes had erected an ore house on the site.

Although the Crown grant was not officially awarded until October, 1894, some construction was begun almost immediately. The first establishment to open for business was probably the Three Forks Hotel, owned by Carpenter, which was operating by mid-June. Here, miners "are getting 'bit' drinks and glad of it," reported the *Miner*. Other businesses established that year included a gent's furnishing store, operated by Pitt Brothers, and a large general store owned by the Galena Trading Company. In addition, Jack Madigan built a livery stable and initiated a freight service.

Unlike Kaslo and New Denver, however, Three Forks' development was slow at first. But the town's fortunes took a decided turn for the better in late April, 1893, when it was announced that the Nakusp & Slocan Railway (N&S) would be constructed from Nakusp, with Three Forks as its terminus. The coming of steel created a great deal of excitement and activity in Three Forks and the town literally boomed.

On October 10, a post office was opened with H.H. Pitt, a future mayor of Sandon, as postmaster. That month alone 35 new houses were built, and the Nakusp *Ledge* reported "log houses going up in every direction and the citizens getting ready for winter." By November the town boasted seven hotels operated by Carpenter, Thomas Norquay, Tirell, Ira Black, Tranery & Devlin, D.C. Weaver and the Slocan Brothers. In addition a man named Becker ran a boarding house. Other businesses included Foster's Restaurant, Pat Burns' butcher shop, Hunter & McKinnon's general store, J. Madigan's livery stable, a blacksmith and a barbershop. R.E. Lemon, the pioneer merchant of Sproat, Nelson and Trail, also had a large general store. In December, Lemon purchased Carpenter's half-interest in the Three Forks Hotel.

Transportation, too, was improving. A daily stage, operated by the Selkirk Transportation Company, ran from Three Forks to Kaslo for $3.50, although the *Ledge* reported that the upper end of the road "is in an almost unpassable condition." By this time Hughes had solidified his position as the principal freighter in the district. On the road between Kaslo and Watson, Hughes operated four-horse freight teams. From Watson to Three Forks a train of 16 pack horses was used, with an additional 16-horse pack train operating from Three Forks to New Denver.

Examining the town-site of Three Forks today, one might be forgiven for wondering where a town of any size could possible have established itself at the forks of Kane, Carpenter and Seaton creeks. The original town-site consisted of 240 lots which were laid out on three benches on the east side of Carpenter Creek. Although each bench rose steeply above one another, they were each, in themselves, fairly level.

During its brief history, Three Forks was a law-abiding community. However, during a dance held there on Saturday, February 23, 1894, the town recorded its first serious altercation when Robert Carlin became incensed at Bert Crane for one reason or another. Rushing over to Lemon's store, Carlin broke in and stole a rifle. Returning to the dance, he then fired at Crane through the building. Although Carlin

*(Right) Scotty Mitchell's store at Bear Lake in 1917. (Opposite page) The remains of the old Nakusp & Slocan right of way near Alamo (New Deluth) in 1989. (Inset) An old rail from the N&S railway abandoned along the right of way. (Below) The first house in Three Forks, 1892. (Inset) All that remains to mark the site of Three Forks today is this sign for the K&S Historic Trail.*

missed, he was promptly arrested and sent to Nelson for trial.

By May, Three Forks was advertising itself in local papers as the terminus of the N&S railway, and "the supply point and center of the Slocan, within easy distance of all mines." By this time lots were being offered at from $100 to $1,000 each.

As the railway neared completion, the town boomed and its future never looked brighter. Then, on June 3, its luck began to change dramatically. About 5 o'clock that Sunday afternoon, a cyclone struck the entire Slocan with suddenness and fury. At Nakusp it destroyed boats and buildings. When the accompanying winds ripped through the valley of Carpenter Creek, it demolished the lower end of town above White's ore house. As the winds approached the upper part of the town, it fanned the ashes from brush burning into flames and threatened to destroy the whole town. The telegraph office and Groneway's store both caught fire, as did the Freddie Lee Hotel. These buildings were only saved by the energetic efforts of the bucket brigade, headed by Police Constable E.M. Sandilands. A building between these houses contained 1,200 pounds of powder. Fortunately, it did not catch fire or "Three Forks would have been blown to the four corners of the globe. Other houses near the North Fork and Seaton Creek were less fortunate, and six of them succumbed to the flames, their owners losing everything. There is no doubt that Three Forks would not be in existence today had it not been for the great downpour of rain which came in just in time to save it."

Residents and businesses had just begun to recover when, on July 24, nature dealt the beleaguered little town a devastating second blow. For some days previously there had been scattered fires in the nearby hills that had caused some apprehension. But on Tuesday, wrote the Nelson *Miner,* "a whirlwind swept over the country, of a greater fury than the memorable storm of June 3rd. It quickly fanned into fierce activity the various fires in the neighbourhood, and sent great tongues of flame leaping and roaring among the dried up pines and firs that clothe the mountain sides. Dense masses of smoke preceded the fires, rolling up the hillsides and filling the valleys. . . . Every house between the Welling ore house on the Kaslo side of Watson and the Slocan Star ore house on the far side of Three Forks was licked up by the angry flames in a few minutes. At Three Forks there is not a single stick left standing."

One of the heaviest losers was George Hughes. His losses of a carload of hay, a carload of oats, a carload of blacksmith coal, 6,000 ore sacks, a bunkhouse, a stable and an ore house was estimated at $20,000. R.E. Lemon lost $10,000, while the Galena Trading Co. lost an estimated $7,000 in merchandise and buildings. Pitt Brothers were also heavy losers at $4,000, their loss made greater by the fact that they had recently brought in furniture and household effects for their families. Crane & Lowes, who had lumber, doors, windows and other materials on hand for an extension to their hotel, also lost $4,000. Wilson & Burns' loses of $4,000 included $2,400 worth of bacon.

"The inhabitants," continued the *Miner,* "saved themselves by creeping into the creek and lying up to their necks in the water and about 30 managed to find safety in an old mining tunnel." Fortunately, there was only one fatality. It occurred when James Forbes, carrying water to throw on a burning cellar, was struck by a falling tree. With his back broken, Forbes suffered excruciating pain for two days before he died.

Despite the fact that nobody in Three Forks had any insurance, the town quickly recovered and, with the aid of Sam Lovett's sawmill, the residents began to rebuild. On August 28 the first saw log was sliced into boards as businessmen, temporarily housed in tents, watched impatiently. A week later, despite running at full capacity, the sawmill was still a long way behind the demand.

Ira Black, whose hotels at Watson and Three Forks had been destroyed by the fire, soon reopened Black's Hotel. Pitt Brothers were rebuilding and G.H. Williams was opening a drug store. The appearance of the town-site, however, apparently left something to be desired, the Nakusp *Ledge* suggesting that the town-site owners should remove the stumps and grade streets. "At present the townsite looks something like a nightmare a man sees after he has supped heavily on boiled lobster and mildewed cheese."

On Sunday, October 27, 1894, the N&S track layers reached Three Forks. The first train from there arrived at Nakusp at midnight of the same day, without fanfare or celebration "to mark the event." The railway buildings at Three Forks included a first-class station, freight shed, two-stall roundhouse, section house, sand house and 2,336 feet of siding. Rolling stock consisted of one first-class passenger car, one combination passenger and baggage car, and about 30 box and flat cars — all supplied by the CPR.

On December 27, Three Forks celebrated its first wedding. The following day the first issue of the Three Forks *Slocan Prospector* made its appearance. Three days later the town was thronged with people for New Year's Day celebrations. Prior to the ball, they enjoyed a wrestling match that took place in Crane & Lowe's hall between packer James Brown and blacksmith Frank Lepert. During this period, building construction was continuing at a feverish pace, and by January, 1895, Wilson & Perdue had opened their new butcher business in competition with Pat Burns. Other establishments included Bartlett & Cronin's Can Can restaurant, A.C. Pierson's laundry and bathhouse, the Pacific Hotel, Archie Grant's hotel, Hunter & McKinnon's general store, the Norquay House, Samuel Green's general store, Henry Giegerich's general store, a drug store and a jail.

The new jail, completed by R.C. Ferguson at a cost of $900, was described as "a comfortable place with five cells, a kitchen and a constable's room." The new town also had its very own red light district. Describing the town at this time, the *Slocan Prospector* wrote: "With its Canadians, Americans, English, Irish, Scotch, French, Italians, Caucasians, Negros and Japanese, Three Forks is getting to be a cosmopolitan, Babalonian town."

Meanwhile, on the N&S line about a mile below Three Forks, a concentrator had been under construction for some time. The main building was constructed in four levels. The lower level covered an area of 153x53 feet, while the top level was 153x31 feet. In addition there was an ore bin with a holding capacity of 2,000 tons. The main building contained crushing and jigging machinery and a Huntington mill, the total capacity of the plant being 100 tons a day. Power was supplied by a Pelton wheel fed by a pipe reaching 1,400 feet up Howson Creek. The N&S had a small siding here.

The small town that developed around the concentrator was given the name of New Duluth by Nathaniel Moore, of Duluth, Minnesota, the concentrator's owner. The Slocan Store Company, also owned by Moore, operated a general store alongside. The concentrator had been established to process ore from the Idaho and Alamo mines, discovered in 1892, and by mid-January, 1895, 15 teams were

(Above) The new concentrator at Alamo in 1919. It was built by Clarence Cunningham to handle ore from the Queen Bess, Sovereign and Wonderful mines.
(Right inset) The remains of an old boiler from the above concentrator in 1990.
(Opposite page) Nature is rapidly taking over the old New Deluth-Alamo town-site, as can be seen in this recent photograph.
(Below) Another view of the building seen on the opposite page.

hauling ore from the latter to the concentrator where it was stockpiled. When the concentrator began operations on February 4, it employed 125 men.

During the two weeks between December 26 and January 8, 54 cars or ore were loaded at the Three Forks depot and at the New Duluth spur. The ore, which had been stockpiled awaiting the arrival of the N&S, included 25 cars from the Idaho; 14 from the Slocan Star, seven from the Cumberland, three from the Reco, three from the Noble Five, two from the Last Chance and one from the Ivanhoe. The total shipment was 810 tons.

As an important railway terminal, Three Forks entered a booming, prosperous period of growth. It was a wide open town where gambling went on around the clock. One night, reported the *Slocan Prospector,* "a card game at Three Forks lasted four days and four nights." Despite this, the town was peaceful and law-abiding and Mr. Allan, the night watchman "finds the town quiet after about 2 a.m. and sometimes for an hour or two before daylight all places are closed and the streets deserted."

By mid-March the New Duluth concentrator was turning out 15 tons of concentrates daily, and it was estimated some 3,000 tons would be shipped out before the season closed. It was now the largest employer in the district, with over 140 men being directly or indirectly on its payroll. A week earlier Moore had announced plans to construct a tramway to the Idaho, Alamo and Cumberland mines as soon as the snow melted. Official notice of his intentions, which appeared in the Nakusp *Ledge* on March 28, read:

"Take notice that we, Nathaniel D. Moore and John Vallance, of Three Forks, B.C., have taken steps to incorporate a company called the 'Slocan Tramway Company,' for the purpose of building and operating a tramway for hauling ore; such tramway to commence at or near the Concentrator, at the mouth of Howson Creek, near Three Forks, West Kootenay, B.C. and proceed up Howson Creek for a distance of about 9,000 feet, and then divide into parts, and proceed by the nearest practical route to the Idaho, St. John, Alamo, Cumberland, and Yakima mines."

In April, 1895, the Three Forks *Slocan Prospector,* which had begun its career in New Denver, moved to Kaslo. Commenting on its movements, the Bonner's Ferry *Herald* wrote: "It is hard to keep track of the Slocan newspapers — they appear to be on wheels. The *Slocan Prospector,* late of New Denver, but later of Three Forks, has moved on to Kaslo and will try that field for awhile." In August, 1895, it moved again; this time to Rossland.

By the end of April, Three Forks had telephone communication, a Ladies' Aid Society had been established, over $100 had been subscribed for the erection of a church, and Frank Locasto, the local barber, had added a billiard table to his establishment, the only one in the Slocan.

At New Duluth, 45 men were working on the tramway, with assurances that the force would be increased to 100 as soon as possible. The T-rails for the tramway were purchased in Calgary, but the B.C. Iron Works of Vancouver had secured the contract for supplying most of the remaining equipment. Constructed on the three rail principle, the tramway required 60 tons of 12-pound rails to complete the job. Six cars, each with a capacity of two tons each, would carry ore from the mines over grades that, in many cases, were a steep 45 percent. The whole system operated on gravity, the loaded car travelling down the tramway pulling up one either empty or containing supplies. The cable used was two inches thick and consisted of 17 strands of extra fine steel.

# SANDON AND CODY

About this time an ominous cloud began to appear on Three Forks' horizon. It had begun innocently enough in the summer of 1892 when John Harris located the Loudoun claim about five miles above Three Forks. After purchasing the Reco mine, Harris concentrated his efforts towards getting it established. Once that was accomplished, however, Harris decided to preempt a town-site in the valley below and applied for a Crown grant to his Loudoun claim, which was awarded in October of that year.

In the spring of 1893, five men, Robert Cunning, Mike Kerlin, Robert Kerlin, Archie Chisholm and Dick Hambley had pitched their tents on the town-site. Cunning and Mike Kerlin then formed a partnership and began cutting logs for a hotel. Once the walls were erected, they split the straightest logs they could find into rough boards, planing the edges with jackknives. In this crude and labour intensive method they produced lumber for the floor and roof.

The town on which their hotel had been erected still remained unnamed. So at a meeting attended by the five men, Cunning suggested they name it after old man John Sandon who had drowned nearby earlier that year, and they all agreed. Thereupon their building, which was the first to be built on the town-site, was christened the Sandon Hotel.

In addition to the five men living on the town-site itself that spring, an estimated 50 miners toiled in the nearby hills. By the fall of 1893 the town's population had increased to between 30 and 40, while some 200 were now employed in the mines. With the dramatic collapse in silver prices later that year, however, most residents left, and Sandon counted as its population only Cunning, Mike Kerlin, Charles Lucason, M.A. Allan and A.L. Roseberry.

In the spring of 1894, silver prices rebounded and miners began to trickle back into the area. Edward R. Atherton, the postmaster who had been burned out at Watson following the fires that raged through the Slocan in the summer of 1894, opened a general store in Sandon. About this time Charles Lundberg of Kaslo opened a second hotel, and Mr. King a third. By May, 1895, Hunter & McKinnon had established a grocery, dry goods and mining supplies store, while Archie Grant was advertising the Grant House in the Nakusp *Ledge,* offering good meals and comfortable rooms. In June, Sandon's fifth hotel was under construction and George Spencer, of Nakusp, was preparing to open a barbershop. On August 1, Sandon gained respectability when a post office was opened in Atherton's store. But, although Sandon would one day outperform Three Forks by leaps and bounds, its initial progress was slow. The main drawback to its early development was the N&S railway. By making Three Forks its terminus, that town boomed and everyone gravitated there.

Now a serious threat to that monopoly was taking shape in the form of the Kaslo & Slocan Railway (K&S), which was wending its way from Kaslo. Unlike the N&S, which had its railhead at Three Forks, the K&S had decided to push its end of steel right into the very heart of the silver-producing mines, and Sandon. By mid-June over 100 men were working on the grade between Three Forks and Sandon, and when the railway reached the latter in October, 1895, it did not bode well for the future prosperity of the former.

(Above) This undated photo of an almost deserted Three Forks was probably taken during its declining years.

(Below) The Nakusp & Slocan Railway depot at Three Forks. In this photo, Carpenter Creek enters from the top, while the town itself was located on the hill to the left.

*(Above) This set of rusting railway wheels was found imbedded in Carpenter Creek at Alamo.*

*(Left) The remains of the Nakusp & Slocan Railway trestle that crossed Carpenter Creek at Alamo. This photo was taken from the concentrator.*

*(Below) A Nakusp & Slocan train at Three Forks on July 1, 1914. The Three Forks town-site was to the left of this view.*

Prior to the arrival of the K&S, ore had to be freighted by pack train or wagon to Three Forks. Now this was no longer necessary. The mines, quite naturally, found it far more convenient to ship with the K&S, than the N&S. The N&S, however, had anticipated this would happen and back in August, 1895, had started work on an extension from Three Forks to Sandon. Track laying began that October and the extension was operating by late November. This switched the centre of activity from Three Forks to Sandon, and while the latter began to flourish, Three Forks was living on borrowed time.

To make matters worst, the owners of the Noble Five decided to construct a tramway from their mine to Cody, a new town-site about a mile beyond Sandon along Carpenter Creek. The town was named for Henry Cody, an old-timer from the Ainsworth district. Except for leaving his name on the town and nearby creek, Cody had little impact on the Slocan, and he later turned his attention to the Lardeau district.

By the summer of 1895, John S. Winter had erected the Cody Creek Hotel. The two-story, 30x50-foot building was the first in Cody, and offered first class accommodation for 60 "tourist and mining men." A.B. Docksteader followed by opening the first general store. By September, Johnson & McKinley were putting the finishing touches on their dry goods store; Thomas Levi had completed his Parks Hotel adjoining the baseball field; W.E. Terrill & Co.'s hotel was nearly ready and Green Brothers had purchased one of the best building lots and were erecting a large general store. The ground was also being graded for four more hotels, owned by McNeill Brothers, G.T. Lundy, McTaggart & Madsen and Adams & Craft, while there was talk of two more being planned. With the Noble Five flume, tramway and concentrator employing 70 men, and nearly 200 lots having been sold by the town-site company, Cody was also beginning to put on important airs.

But the activity at Cody paled with the events occurring at Sandon. On September 26, 1896, Robert Lowery, publisher of the Nakusp *Ledge,* started the Sandon *Paystreak* with J.J. Langstaff, the one-time publisher of the Trout Lake *Topic,* as editor. Its first issue is filled with construction notes of Sandon: "The sound of the carpenter's hammer is everywhere heard in Sandon and building operations are being vigorously prosecuted on every side. Some very tasty dwelling houses are being erected and the liveliest and busiest town in the Slocan country is every day assuming a more urban-like appearance than is usually met with in a mining center. Some 20 buildings, dwellings and otherwise are now under construction and still more are contemplated."

Hotels already operating or under construction included Robert Cunning's Sandon Hotel, Ira Black's Hotel, George LeDuke's Palace House, Switzer & Company's Hotel Kootenay, Clair & Thompson's Thistle Hotel, Robert & Neil MacDonald's Hotel Balmoral, Chisholm & Walmsley's Star Hotel, John Buckley's Clifton House, Moore & Orando's Hotel Ivanhoe and the Hotel Bryan. The Thistle, previously known as the Grant House, one of the oldest in town, even boasted its own bowling alley. In addition to these hotels, George Hambly was erecting a hotel mid-way between Sandon and Cody.

Sandon's other establishments included: Leighton & Williams real estate and mining office; J.H. Durfee, watchmaker; Fitzgerald & Day's Sandon Bottling Co.; M.L. Grimmett, barrister; Bartlett Brothers, packers and forwarders; H.C. Holden, painter; F.J. Donaldson, druggist; J.C. Hayes' Slocan Hardware Co.; J.S. Reeder's

Sandon Laundry; J.R. Cameron's Kootenay Mercantile Tailoring Co.; Hunter & McKinnon's general store; Hamilton Byers hardware store; Nick Palorcia's shoe store and Crawford's blacksmith shop. Sandon also boasted a school, cigar store, post office, stationery store, transfer company and two butcher shops, one operated by Pat Burns, who also had stores in Rossland, Nelson, Kaslo, Pilot Bay, Three Forks and Cody. The second was operated by the West Kootenay Butcher Company of Nelson.

Trying not to be outdone during this feverish phase of construction at Sandon and Cody, Three Forks and New Duluth forged boldly ahead. By July, 1895, the tramway had been completed to the New Duluth concentrator and several new buildings, including houses for the families of the superintendent, manager and workmen had been erected. By September the concentrator was turning out a car load of Alamo concentrates daily, averaging about 125 ounces. In November, Nathaniel Moore and John Vallance completed their residences, and a large building had been erected to serve as offices for the concentrator and the mines that supplied it with raw material.

Meanwhile, a mile down the track, Three Forks was still relatively robust. On August 5, 1895, the town celebrated the birth of a son to Mr. and Mrs. Thomas, the first baby born in Three Forks. The same month saw the completion of a building to be used as a church and school. Mr. McDowell was the first school teacher. In September, R.D. Cameron of Winnipeg established a branch store in Three Forks, and the following month the Pacific Hotel, one of the largest in the Slocan, was reported to be doing a good business. D.C. Weaver had already opened his new hotel and in early November the Miner's Exchange Hotel opened its doors.

But, even at this early date, Three Forks was beginning to feel the pressure of its burgeoning neighbour, Sandon. Back in July, Sam Lovett had moved his sawmill from Three Forks to Sandon. In November, C.M. Wilson moved his assay office there, while J.B. Wilson closed his Three Forks store and concentrated on his Kaslo branch. In December, W.E. Terrill & Co. secured a building lot in Sandon. Later the same month, the 20-room Palace Hotel was put up for sale.

During the winter of 1896 and throughout 1897, Sandon was the scene of phenomenal growth. By December, 1896, two charter banks had been established there; the Bank of British Columbia had been first, followed by the Bank of British North America. By the summer of 1897, Sandon boasted 17 hotels, seven general stores, five carpenter shops, five mining agencies, five laundries, five gent's furnishing stores, four saloons, four restaurants, four barber shops, three doctors, three butcher shops, three bakeries, three fruit stores, three tailors, three jewellers, two assay offices, two law offices, two hardware stores, two groceries, two boot and shoe makers, two bottling works, two drug stores, two millinery stores, two banks, two railways, and two newspapers and printing offices. There was also a dentist, insurance agency, packer, brewery, news agency, book store, tin shop, dress maker, sawmill, taffy puller and livery stable. Sandon also had the most advanced electric light and power system in North America at the time. Water for the generators was flumed in from the surrounding mountain creeks. (One of the generators still provides electricity for the few homes remaining in Sandon.)

Sandon's second newspaper, the *Mining Review*, made its appearance on June 12, 1897. In response to its rival, the *Paystreak* wrote: "Cliffe & Co. have opened a bookstore in Sandon. They have also started a rancified advertising sheet, which

*(Left) The remains of the Sandon City Hall in 1984.*
*(Opposite page) This view of Sandon was taken before the Virginia Block, next to the brick building, had collapsed. Plans are now underway to repair and restore the brick building.*
*(Opposite page, inset) The Sandon Hotel shown here was rebuilt after the fire of 1900. The original Sandon Hotel was constructed of logs and was the first hotel in Sandon.*
*(Below) A view along narrow Reco Avenue in Sandon in 1898. Two years after this photo was taken a disastrous fire completely destroyed the business section. Sandon was quickly rebuilt, but it never again attained the stature it had before the fire.*

is principally devoted to puffing their own business and ancient history. The paper, which is misnamed the *Mining Review,* looks like a starved tramp, and will not make it necessary to organize a fire department to protect the universe."

So much for the niceties of a frontier "Welcome Wagon." In response to this criticism, the *Mining Review* wrote: "We are disposed to let the public decide on the merits or demerits, as the case may be, of the issue. We have neither time, space nor inclination to waste on fishwife literature."

Amidst all the new construction, the residents found time to begin the formation of a Fire Brigade. It got its first test on January 7, 1897, when fire broke out in the Clifton House about 1 a.m. after an oil lamp was accidentally upset. The fire alarm was sounded and after some delay the Fire Brigade arrived and extinguished the flames. The club room, at the back of the bar was scorched a little, but beyond giving the guests a severe scare, only about $100 in damage was done.

Six months later, Levi's Parks Hotel in nearby Cody would suffer a far worst fate, when a fire, started under "peculiar circumstances" completely destroyed the building. Mr. and Mrs. Levi, an aged couple, were both asleep when the fire started. It was caused when a lamp in an incubator underneath the building exploded. By the time the Levi's were aware of the fire the flames had made considerable headway. Mrs. Levi, a heavy woman, jumped from an upstairs window to safety. Despite being badly shaken, she then carried a heavy ladder on her shoulder and placed it up to the window so her husband could escape.

The fire destroyed the Levi's entire worldly possessions, a serious matter at their age. In true frontier fashion, however, the ladies of Sandon took up a subscription and raised funds to aid the couple. In addition, a dance was held in the Cody Creek Hotel for their benefit. In total $200 was raised, and Levi was soon operating a hotel from a building he leased near the brewery.

These fires showed how susceptible wooden frontier towns were to conflagration, and prompted the *Paystreak* to complain about the lack of government funding for essential services such as fire and police protection. In an editorial the newspaper stated that the government annually received $4,000 for liquor and trade licences alone, yet they contributed virtually nothing back to the town. For fire protection, complained the paper, the town had to purchase the hose reel and other equipment through public subscription. Police protection was scarcely any better. "The government has been paying up to the present time, the munificent sum of $30 per month to a constable, and had not the citizens of Sandon supplemented it by $60 we would have been without police protection, as no one can live on $30 per month."

Sandon was growing so rapidly that sanitation had also become a pressing concern. "Last winter Sandon was a town of sufficient importance to merit closer attention to a means of disposing of rubbish and offal. But nothing was done, either during the winter or summer. After almost two years accumulation of rubbish has been piled at the back door and in the alleyways, along comes the sanitary inspector and holds up his hands in horror at such uncleanliness, part of which he cannot see for the snow had already covered it up. He immediately gets in and threatens the people with all the terrors of the law." The solution, editorialized the paper, incorporate as a city and control their own affairs. But incorporation would not come for some time yet.

Despite the new construction, mining activities and political growing pains of a new town, Sandon still found time to participate in sports. In December, 1896, construction had been completed on an ice rink, and on December 11, the Sandon Curling Club was formed. On January 27, 1897, the first game of curling ever played in the Slocan was witnessed by a large number of interested spectators, many of whom had never seen the sport before. On February 13, Sandon hosted Kaslo in a curling match, which was won by the locals 20 to 11. A week later Sandon travelled to Kaslo for a rematch, playing for the District Medal. Sandon overcame the disadvantage of playing on Kaslo's 15-foot longer rink and emerged victorious.

Back in Sandon, meanwhile, a hockey match played between the Blacks and Whites resulted in a 6-3 victory for the Blacks. On February 24 the Sandon hockey team travelled to Kaslo for a game, winning 5-2. In early March, Sandon's hockey team played against Rossland and Kaslo, winning both games and the emblematic cup. Other sports included baseball, lacrosse and tennis, all established in May, 1897.

Sandon was experiencing unprecedented prosperity and growth, as evidenced by the CPR passenger totals for the first six months of 1897: January 341, February 468, March 695, April 730, May 1,002 and June 1,040.

Cody, too, was progressing. On May 1, 1897, a post office was opened in Docksteader's store. Elsewhere, a number of new homes were being built and the streets were being graded. According to the *Paystreak,* "All the business houses are doing well and the prospects are bright for a good summer." Bennett & Carbary were erecting a new hotel on Cody Avenue, while Bongard & Peickart had purchased S.T. Lundy's hotel at Cody. After refurnishing and refitting it throughout, it was reopened as the Noble Five Hotel.

Even Three Forks was enjoying a brief resurgence. "People are coming into Three Forks every day," wrote the *Paystreak.* "There is not an empty residence in town, and several new business houses have been opened."

But, by July, 1897, a sudden drop in the price of silver checked all speculation and the boom was over. Although several of the older claims like the Payne, Ruth and Whitewater, forged ahead and became heavy shippers, no new properties attained special prominence during the year. Several others, such as the Queen Bess, Charleston, Ivanhoe and Last Chance, reported having good ore chutes now in site.

Sandon was incorporated in December, 1897. The city's first mayor was E.R. Atherton, who was elected by acclamation. Likewise, the first city council, consisting of aldermen Robert Cunning, Alexander Crawford, Stuart Mighton, Robert Broddy, Charles Hunter and John Switzer, had run unopposed. By this time Sandon boasted 24 hotels and 23 saloons. Little bragging was done about the 115 "ladies of ill-repute" who resided in Sandon, however. The population was about 5,000, with an additional 2,000 or so miners living in the surrounding hills.

During its heyday, Sandon was wide-open and rip-roaring. Whisky flowed freely and gambling continued around the clock. The *Paystreak* described the scene:

"In the West, many men are in the habit of coming to town every little while and blowing in all their money upon yellow liquor, the green cloth and the women in red. After a few days of hilarity they usually sober up broke, grow repentant, and then hit the hills for another stake, fully determined that they will never again sip the booze, shuffle the cards or trifle with the painted faces of commercial love. As time goes along and their pile grows bigger, the memory of past misery fades, and back they come to camp and history repeats itself."

Unlike many historic mining towns in British Columbia, Sandon never had a

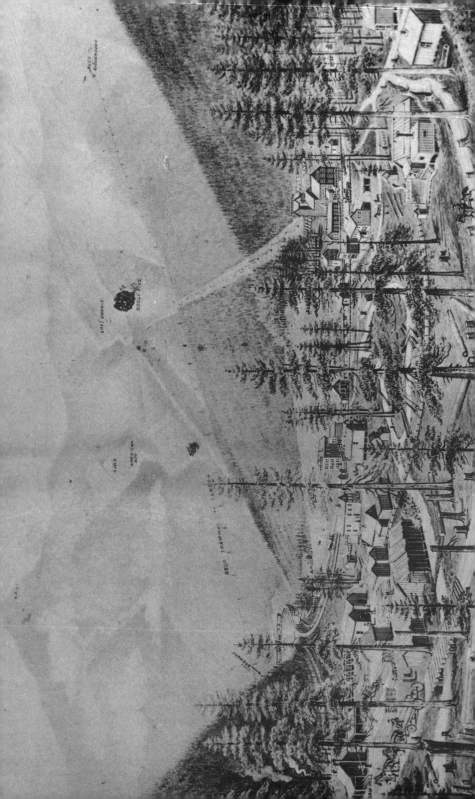

*(Above) This photo of Mr. & Mrs. Samuel Green with their children Howard, Roland and Edith was taken in Kaslo c1904.*
*(Left) Sandon's last remaining fire hydrant.*
*(Opposite page) This sketch of Cody was made during its heyday and shows the Noble Five concentrator and tramway, the remains of which can still be seen today.*
*(Below) The Tin Cup Cafe and another building at the upper end of Sandon.*

Chinatown. The reason was simple; the Chinese were despised throughout West Kootenay. In its early days, hotels in Ainsworth and Nelson would proudly advertise the fact that they did not employ Chinese. Sandon, and other communities throughout the Slocan, were composed of immigrants from all over the world, yet only the Chinese were despised. This apparently stemmed from the fact that the Chinese were willing to work for far less then other workers, and thereby lowered everyone's standard of living.

The Chinese made their first appearance in Sandon in 1898 when four orientals were hired to work in the mines. This was resented by the other miners, and they decided to do something about it. Rounding up the four men, they "escorted" them out of Sandon and made it clear they were not welcome in the region. As a result of this action, two miners were sent to Nelson for trial. This prompted Robert Lowery, in the New Denver *Ledge* to editorialize:

"During the past few weeks the Slocan country has again emphatically declared itself opposed to the employment of Chinese, especially among the miners. Those working in the camps around Sandon have been rustled out of the district, and it is hoped their fellows will have sufficient 'savvy' not to tempt Providence further in the matter."

Lowery considered it unfortunate that two miners had been arrested for "getting rid of the obnoxious and unwholesome Mongolians," since, according to him, no violence had occurred. Lowery went on to state: "Slocan has time and time again pronounced against the Chinese and their bilious decoctions, and the mine-owners are in large measure to blame for the present situation. No one wishes to antagonize the law, but the fact must be impressed upon the employers of labor, that the Chinese are not wanted. Let it be said that one spot in B.C. — the Slocan, and the richest of them all — is free from the contaminating influence of the unhallowed and unwashed sons of China."

The remainder of 1898 and the first five months of 1899 were relatively uneventful in Sandon. Then, in June, 1899, the miners went on strike.

Prior to the walkout, miners worked 10 hours a day for which they were paid $3.50. However, when legislation was passed making the eight-hour day mandatory, the mine owners felt compelled to offer only $3 for the shorter period. The miners refused to work for the lower rate and a protracted strike followed.

As the months dragged on, the mine owners offered a compromise: $3.50 per day for the "machine operating" miners and $3.25 a day for "hand" miners. This was rejected by the union, which continued to demand $3.50 across the board and were only prepared to sign a 30-day agreement. Finally, in the spring of 1900, nine months after it began, both sides agreed to a wage of $3.25. The strike proved to be a serious economic blow to the city, as, while it lasted, many miners and residents left Sandon for the Klondike. Before Sandon could recover, the 1900 fire occurred. This two events marked the beginning of Sandon's decline.

# THE GREAT SANDON FIRE

The fire started at Spencer's Opera House shortly after midnight on May 4, 1900. A short time earlier, a capacity crowd had been entertained there by the play "Bitter Atonement," and the *Paystreak* said it seemed as if the fire was "a sequel to the play."

Despite written reports by modern historians that the fire had been caused during intermission when a careless actor tossed a burning cigarette into a wastepaper basket, the Sandon newspaper does not confirm this. In fact, the *Paystreak* states: "Though the fire was first noticed at Spencer's, it cannot be said to have been the result of carelessness on the part of any one in connection with the show as it was found to be on the outside between the building and Thos. Brown's."

Regardless of where the fire originated, by the time the fire brigade and concerned residents reached the scene it was already too late. The opera house was ablaze and the flames were rapidly spreading along the tightly packed streets of tinder dry wooden buildings. In an effort to prevent the fire from spreading beyond the business district, several buildings in its path were blown up. The strategy failed, however, and, despite the valiant efforts of volunteers and a reservoir with a capacity some 60,000 gallons of water, the extreme heat soon ignited stores above the Presbyterian and Methodist churches and quickly spread to Sunnyside on the hillside. Residents were forced to abandon their homes and flee with anything they could carry. Hundreds of men, women and children were thrust from their homes. Seeking the safety of higher ground, they watched horrified as all their worldly possessions went up in smoke.

The inferno was not brought under control until late morning, by which time it had destroyed most of Sandon's business district. All that remained was the brick lower story of Atherton's warehouse, Folliott & McMillan's factory and old blacksmith shop adjoining it, Hunter's warehouse, the electric light power house and some residences. The buildings verging on the burned district, which were saved, included: the K&S depot, the stores of Henry Giegerich & H. Byers, Crawford & Grimmitt's livery stable, W.H. Lilly's house, P. Burns refrigerator, D.J. Robertson's warehouse, and on Sunnyside the residences of C. Cliffe and William Richards.

Harris and Kelly were by far the biggest losers. Their properties included: Reco Hotel ($30,000), Virginia Block ($18,000), Goodenough Hotel ($12,000), Reco Laundry ($6,000), Bank Building ($5,000) and various other buildings totalling $100,000, none of which were insured.

Hotels destroyed by the fire included: Sandon ($18,000), Exchange ($11,000), Clifton ($9,000), Klondike ($4,500), Palace ($4,500), Miner's ($3,000), Star ($3,000), Kootenay ($2,000), Vancouver ($2,000), Balmoral ($1,500) and Thistle. Of these, the Sandon was insured for $2,000 and the Palace for $1,000; the remainder carried no insurance.

Other major business buildings destroyed included: E.R. Atherton & Co. ($30,000), Hunter Brothers ($25,000), H.H. Pitts ($8,000), Sandon *Mining Review* office and printing plant ($7,500), P. Burns & Co. ($7,000), Central Music Hall ($5,000), F.J. Donaldson's Drug Store ($5,000), Main Brothers Liquor Store ($5,000), McQueen's Drug Store ($5,000), Sandon Fire Hall ($5,000), G.D. McMartin's Barbershop ($3,500) and the Bank of B.C. ($3,000). Both churches, numerous residences, and other businesses were also destroyed.

The losses listed by the *Paystreak* on the day of the fire totalled $435,350, but the paper cautioned that this amount would climb well over half a million as no allowance had been made for the destruction of roads, sidewalks, flumes, etc. When the final figures were in, the total damage approached $750,000, most of which was uninsured.

But the citizens of Sandon were nothing if not resourceful. The day after the fire gambling tables were operating among the still smouldering ruins, while residents vowed to rebuild Sandon bigger and better than before. Within a week nearly every

(Left) A small bridge leads to one of the trails in Sandon.

(Opposite page, top) What was once the concentrator and office buildings for the Ivanhoe mine are now being used by Dickenson Mines.

(Opposite page, bottom) This old GMC truck is parked in a field at Sandon.

(Below) Sandon, the day after the destructive fire of May 4, 1900. (Inset) The City of Sandon incorporation seal stands about two feet high.

businessman in Sandon had secured some location in which to reopen and canvas tents and telephone shacks had taken the place of the substantial buildings that had formerly graced Reco Avenue.

"The Dawson-like appearance of the town," wrote the *Paystreak,* "with windowless stores, saloons under canvas, black-jack in the streets, etc., etc., does not seem to effect the spirits of the community and everyone is going in for rebuilding with all the energy possible." In the meantime, the Bank of B.C. was occupying the building next to Robertson's furniture store. F.J. Donaldson had reopened in the same building. The post office was temporarily located in the O.K. Farmer warehouse, while E.R. Atherton was conducting business from a large tent alongside his old warehouse. Hunter Brothers were also operating from a tent on their old lot, while Parham, McMartin, Cliffe, Melvin, Sandilands and the Stein Brothers were camped on the K&S ground near the depot.

Two weeks after the fire the *Paystreak* printed a letter from J.M. Harris, who had been out of town when the fire occurred. Since returning, Harris had read criticism regarding the unsatisfactory working of his water system in the Associated Press. To counter this denunciation, Harris stated that he had made a diligent investigation upon his return and found that his equipment was not at fault. He wrote: "I find that both the water systems were supplied all the time with an abundance of water, and that one system lost its pressure only after a number of lines of hose had been permitted to burn up while attached, leaving the hydrants to flow unchecked in the street."

The following week, Frank Sewell, Sandon's Fire Chief, printed an angry rebuttal to Harris' claim. "From whom did Mr. Harris receive his information? From reliable sources, or was the theory father to the thought? The water from the hydrant in front of the Reco Hotel played out in just half an hour from the time of the first alarm, and if the fire spread with such ra(p)idity that in half an hour the hydrant supplying 'a number of hoses' became too hot to stand by, thus causing failure of the upper hydrant, any man outside of the brigade could be excused for deserting the hydrant and forgetting to shut it down. But if the hydrants were left open, how was it that they were not still running in the morning when the ruins became sufficiently cool to reach them? Mr. Harris has been misinformed."

After admitting that no fault could be found with the service of the Sandon Water and Light Company, claiming it had been found to be the best natural pressure service in the province, Sewell continued his attack on Harris. "He charges the fire brigade with being remiss in their duty; but since the citizens who were present during the fire do not so believe, the opinion of Mr. Harris, who was some thousands of miles away, bears little weight. There has been no moment during the last two and a half years that all the apparatus has not been ready for instant service — except during practice. The fire station doors have never been fastened, and on that particular night, were wide open. The alarm bell rope was in the same place it has always been since the alarm bell was hung.

"In view of the great loss which Mr. Harris has sustained, his statements might be excused if the brigade consisted of paid members. This was not the case. On the contrary, half a dozen members lost everything they possessed endeavouring to perform their duty, whilst if they had deserted their posts which they had voluntarily assumed, for only a few moments, they might have saved everything, and the morning would not have found them as it did without a suit of clothes.

Personally I may have made many mistakes, but if so I have paid for them just as severely as Mr. Harris, and Mr. Harris may criticize my actions as much as he chooses, it is a matter of indifference to me, but I do not intend to stand quietly by and hear him vilify the unpaid members of a volunteer brigade who risked their lives and lost their all that night in attempting what proved to be an impossible task. I am borne out by every unprejudiced man in Sandon present at the fire when I say that Mr. Harris' strictures on the fire department, both verbal and printed, are entirely uncalled for and in the worst possible taste."

Meanwhile, the residents and businessmen of Sandon were almost unanimous that they should take advantage of the destruction caused by the fire to have Sandon re-surveyed. The plan was to establish a new 60-foot-wide street down the middle of the gulch, using the flume as a sewer and subway for the water mains, electric lights and telephone wires. To enable this scheme to work, a trustee would be appointed to take over the lots and issue script to the owner to the extent of the assessed value. These would then be applied to the value of the new lot. Because of the possibility of a re-survey, no permanent buildings were under construction, as everyone waited to see whether they should re-build along old narrow Reco Avenue or the proposed new road.

On May 19, the *Paystreak* reported that provincial land surveyor A.R. Heyland had almost completed the re-survey of the Sandon town-site. Harris, one of the largest property holders, stated he "was willing to consider any reasonable proposition to which the other property holders would be agreeable. . . . Outside of himself and Sproat there were only eight property holders along the hill side of Reco Avenue."

Harris' lots from the Broddy Block to the lower end of town would be made practically valueless by the change, and it was from there that he had obtained the majority of his rental revenue. However, Harris was ready and willing to sacrifice this property as he expected to be partially reimbursed by the enhanced value the new street would give to the properties he owned in the area between the flume and the CPR.

The land owners on the opposite side of the street were not to be materially affected. They would retain the same size lot as previously, the re-survey would simply move these lots back from the flume 50 feet.

On Tuesday evening, June 5, the Sandon city council met to discuss the proposed changes to Reco Avenue. The vote ended in a tie, with three in favour of a new 60-foot road, and three opposed. Mayor Pitts, who was called upon to cast the deciding vote, was also opposed. Reporting on the decision, the *Paystreak* wrote: "The council decided on Tuesday evening that the old street should remain as it was unless the property holders on Reco Avenue donated land to widen it. J.M. Harris now offers to give 10 feet off the front of his lots for this purpose if the city will grade that part of it along by the skating rink."

With the matter of the road apparently decided upon, construction of new buildings finally began, the *Paystreak* noting: "Like the mythological Phoenix, it (Sandon) rises from the ashes, larger and better than before." Among those engaged in construction were Mrs. Egan, whose three story, 30x50-foot hotel was taking shape on the lower skating rink lot. The Sandon Miners' Union had selected a lot below the Reco Hotel for a union hall and hospital, while the Filbert building was rapidly going ahead.

(Above) The concentrator of the Noble Five Mining Company, showing the tramway up the mountainside.
(Opposite page) The remains of the Noble Five concentrator today. Although a lot of new growth has taken place, the tramway clearing is still visible just above the buildings.
(Below) The remains of heavy machinery that was contained in the Noble Five concentrator building. The building in the background is the white one seen in the above photo.

Of all the new construction being undertaken, however, none matched Harris' new Reco Hotel. It was being built in the 60x80-foot building that had previously been occupied by Hammond Brothers. The ground floor had a 24x60-foot dining room with a kitchen, pantry, store rooms and ice chest. Carpenters were hard at work constructing half a dozen dining boxes for the accommodation of guests who desired privacy. A hall and stairway separated the dining room with the other side containing a barroom, billiard room, club rooms and a barbershop. Upstairs the building contained 20 large, well lighted, airy bedrooms, with a parlour in the front and rear. Elsewhere, Robert Cunning was erecting a new 60x60-foot Sandon Hotel.

However, as all this new construction got seriously underway, it was soon realized that the builders were ignoring the councils dictum to follow the old Reco Avenue, and instead, were building along the proposed new road. At first, there was no interference, but on July 6 the problem came to a head when an emergency meeting of the city council was held in Mayor Pitt's store.

All had apparently been progressing smoothly along the new road until Cunning began construction of his Sandon Hotel. He too, followed the new road, but in order to do so, his foundation projected 10 feet into old Reco Avenue. After receiving complaints, Chief Stubbs summoned Cunning to appear in court on July 5 to answer a charge of obstructing a highway. However, the case was adjourned and the council was summoned to resolve the problem.

After debating the pros and cons of the case, the council concluded that it was not in a position to either open the new street or abandon the old one, although all present except Alderman Buckley favoured the new street. Mayor Pitts apparently became so angry that he tendered his resignation as mayor. However, since it was an emergency meeting and not a general one, the resignation could not be considered until the next regular meeting on July 16. But, two days before the council was due to meet, the *Paystreak* announced that Cunning had rearranged his foundation so that his hotel no longer extended into Reco Street. However, since Cunning wanted it to remain 60 feet deep, it now extended 10 feet into the new street instead.

By August, much of Sandon's business district had been rebuilt; but it would never again reach the lofty heights it had attained prior to the fire. Many residents who were bankrupted by the long strike and the fire left Sandon and never returned. With wide-open gambling fast disappearing, even the very fabric of the city itself was changing.

"Second dealers in Sandon are at a discount now," wrote the *Paystreak*. "Their occupation is gone. No more the little stacks of reds and blues pass back and forth at the behest of the fickle goddess of fortune. No more the roulette wheel burr nor the faro king reigns where dead game sports bet 'em to the rafters and lucky ikes double shoot the turf. The seductive game of black (jack) no longer entertains the young man brave and 'licky,' and 'Hit the kitty,' 'I'm fat,' 'Smashthesonofa ____' 'That's the baby,' are but a mournful memory of days gone by.

"It's all off now. Chips that pass in the night are only valuable as souvenirs, and the agitation for the free and unlimited coinage of poker checks is only a matter of ancient history. The dealers, boosters, chair-warmers, pluggers, cappers, professional rubber-necks, markers, rimmers, crimpers, short card men, Montana sleeve artists and other methods of the sporting fraternity will have to turn their backs on the classic shades of Silver City, and with heavy-hearts and tear-stained eyes hit the long array of ties to the land of exile. The great moral wave has overtaken them — in Sandon."

But although Sandon had taken on a new morality, it did not suppress its ingrained bigotry and hatred for its Chinese citizens. On October 20, in an editorial, the *Paystreak* noted: "The slant-eyed heathen from the land of hop fiends and dead missionaries has at last fastened himself on Sandon. Jim Kee, an Oriental from Whitewater, has purchased a patch of ground at the lower end of the K&S addition and together with several other Chinamen is proceeding to start a market garden.

"These are the first Chinamen to permanently settle in Sandon, but they will no doubt be followed by many others in the near future and a regular Chinatown, with its opium joints, fan tan layouts, bad smells and all the other disgusting appurtenances will soon become a part of the Silver City of the Slocan."

As the months passed, Sandon's population began to slide. In December, the Bank of B.C. announced that it would amalgamate with the Canadian Bank of Commerce on January 1, 1901. Construction was still continuing, but it had slowed considerably. Then, during the first week of June, residents of Sandon witnessed a preview of what would, 54 years later, virtually destroy the city.

For several days in early June it was very hot and the deep snow that had accumulated in the mountains the previous winter began to melt rapidly. On Friday, Saturday and Sunday, the rate of melting was estimated at two feet per day. Carpenter and Sandon creeks swelled to overflowing as the residents watched anxiously.

On Sunday night a big jam of logs dammed Sandon Creek, forcing the water to form a new channel down the Slocan Star road. The torrent swept everything before it as it went around the obstruction, destroying the road and piling up debris to the depth of over 10 feet when it re-entered the creek at the Sandon Forwarding Company's stables. Here the debris carried by the water formed another dam, and once again the water sought another route, this time rushing down the back street, flooding all cellars from Reco Avenue down.

Responding to the emergency, men were soon on the scene. Working frantically with planks, rocks and sacks of gravel, they constructed a barrier to divert the flow away from the business section. Elsewhere, others were busy clearing away the blockage in front of the Sandon Forwarding Company stables. Finally, about 11 o'clock, the obstruction had been cleared and the water roared through its proper channel once more. Unfortunately, the danger was far from over, and men stationed near the mouth of the flume had to clear away one jam after another. Part of the flume cribbing gave way in many places and, blocking the channel, had to be blown up with dynamite many times during the day.

In the afternoon a big jam occurred under the Denver House, which straddled the creek. This building had been a menace every since it was constructed, and the majority of residents had wanted it removed. Each time there was a freshet, a blockage occurred here, but the one on Monday was the worse yet. A log carried down the raging current knocked out the centre support, tore out a section of cribbing and began to form a dam. For a time things looked serious for the rest of the town. Only hard work by a group of men was able to clear away the obstructions, but not before the hind portion of the building was seriously undermined. For a time it was feared the building would collapse in the centre, which would prove disastrous. But a large log was found and after being securely anchored with ropes, served as a breakwater against further undermining of the building.

About 7 o'clock another jam occurred under the bridge at the power house, but,

*(Above) Three West Kootenay pioneers; Robert Green, Henry Giegerich and Samuel Green.*

*(Right) The Martin residence was the last building standing in Three Forks in 1975. Today there are none.*

*(Opposite page, top) This building, which housed Henry Giegerich's general store and Hamilton Byers' hardware store stood on Reco Avenue, but survived the fire of 1900.*

*(Opposite page, bottom) This moss-covered building, on the hill behind the Alamo concentrator, was once used as a stable.*

*(Below) These teams of horses, seen here in Three Forks, were employed in constructing the CPR right of way from Three Forks to Kaslo. By this time, Three Forks was virtually dead.*

despite the dangers, men went to work and pried up the bridge to let a big stump through. The cribwork nearby was badly shattered, and A. Osborne's stable, the curling and skating rinks were flooded. Standing waist deep in the water, Johnston and Craig constructed a barrier of planks and old pipes. Finally, the immediate danger point passed. "Fortunately the electric light plant sustained no injury," reported the *Mining Review,* "and the misfortune of darkness with the flood was averted."

Although watchmen were posted to warn of danger, very few residents slept on Monday night. About 3 a.m. a blockage occurred in the flume near the Catholic Church. To loosen up the stumps it was necessary to remove part of the flume covering. In clearing away this jam some of the flume bottom was carried away. Two hours later another jam occurred at Atherton's store. Although this was soon cleared away, once again more flume planks were washed away, permitting the splashing water to crumble away the earth and weaken the flume itself. Huge rocks and old safes were rolled into the holes and the splashing ceased for a time. Although Tuesday was a day of anxiety, the water level began to receed and the danger was gradually over.

This was another setback for the town and its population continued to slide. The declining population reached crises proportion in September, 1902, when Sandon found itself without a city council.

"Sandon is up against a unique dilemma," reported the *Paystreak.* "It has no city council and according to the deputy-attorney-general, there is no power to elect or appoint one. The whole municipal machinery is inoperative and there is no power in the hands of what is left of the city council to start it up again. . . . No accounts have been paid for three months. The policeman and the city clerk are without salaries. The school teacher has $285 coming to him, with no way of getting it. The school is without fuel and there is no money appropriated to pay for the same. No tax rate for 1902 has been struck and there is no power to strike one, in consequence of which not a cent in taxes has been collected for the current year. There is no police commission, no license commission and no finance committee."

Sandon's woes began on January 15, 1902, when the new council, consisting of Mayor Robert Cunning and aldermen Thomas Brown, Robert Jalland, Ernest Stein, T.B. Folliott, Thomas Duffy and E.A. Cameron were elected. All went well for the first few months and the affairs of the city were conducted "in a capable and business-like manner." In April, however, the council began to disintegrate. That month Alderman Duffy moved to Grand Forks and Alderman Stein moved to Portland, Oregon. The council now consisted of a mayor and four aldermen. Because there was a lack of qualified people still remaining in Sandon to fill the vacancies, the council did not accept the resignations until absolutely necessary. When, in July, Alderman Jalland moved to Edmonton, the council, with a bare quorum, was forced to act.

On July 7 it was advertised that an election would take place on July 21. As feared, no nominations were presented for election. As the law allowed in such emergencies, the council then appointed two men, Crawford and Osborne, to act as aldermen. On July 26, Folliott's sudden death deprived the council of a quorum, leaving only Mayor Cunning and aldermen Brown and Cameron on the old council. On August 4, the council, with its two new members, was due to meet; but Crawford and Osborne refused to appear. This meant the council was without a quorum, and was unable to call for another election, make any new appointments, or even declare the seats of ex-aldermen Jalland and Folliott vacant.

On August 13, C.E. Lyons, Sandon's City Clerk, wrote to the attorney general's department requesting a warrant for holding a new election. After a wait of nearly a month, Deputy Atty. Gen. H.A. MacLean replied. Unfortunately, the city council found itself in a rather unique situation. MacLean informed Lyons that they had already had their election. It was unfortunate that no one had been elected, but that fact did not give the lieutenant-governor-in-council the power to intervene. As for Alderman Jalland moving from the province, this did not automatically vacate his seat until he had been absent for three months and the council had passed a resolution declaring the office vacant. MacLean acknowledged that, because the council lacked a quorum, it was unable to pass such a resolution. Similarly, the death of Folliott did not vacate his seat. Once again a resolution had to be passed by council, and once again, because it lacked a quorum, the council was powerless to act.

"What the outcome of the matter will be," wrote the *Paystreak,* "remains to be seen. The case is no doubt without precedent and if the deputy-attorney-general's position is unassailable there is to be no outcome. The case cannot improve with time as the council, having no quorum, can not make any arrangements for an election now or on January 15 next, when the normal election should take place."

On September 27, the *Paystreak* announced that Sandon would get its council. The letter from H.A. MacLean read, in part: "It is quite clear that the lieutenant-governor-in-council cannot issue a warrant authorizing the holding of an election of aldermen in the place of Messrs. Jalland and Folliott, as the offices of these aldermen have not been declared vacant. An order-in-council will be passed authorizing the holding of an election to fill the vacancies created by the resignation of Messrs. Duffy and Stein."

C.E. Lyons received the necessary warrant in late October and an election was called for October 30. In its issue of November 1, the *Paystreak* announced that Sandon finally had its council, Charles Walmsley and Dr. W.E. Gomm agreeing to accept the nominations to fill the two vacancies. Sandon's political crisis was finally over, but it was still a town in decline.

On a hot July day in 1906 another disastrous fire burned out a residential section of upper Sandon. This fire was started by a four-year-old boy playing with matches in his mother's bedroom. A breeze blew a lace curtain over the match and flames raced up the curtain, setting the papered wall on fire. The frightened youngster crawled under the bed. Knowing the house could not be saved, his parents and sister were huddled outside watching the inferno. Suddenly the sister realized her brother was not with them, and dashed back into the house. She was able to drag him to safety, but her hands were badly burned.

Although the volunteer fire department was soon on the scene, the fire spread rapidly. The K&S train had just arrived and the train crew at once joined the fire fighters. At one point the firemen were forced to retreat, leaving much of their equipment to the mercy of the flames. In all, 18 houses and the Miners' Union Hospital were destroyed. Fortunately, the only casualty was a dog that ran into a blazing building and was trapped when the door blew shut.

The First World War took a heavy toll of Sandon's young men, many of whom never returned. By this time silver prices were gradually falling and many of the

*(Right) An interior view of the Sandon Museum.*
*(Opposite page) Alamo's best preserved building is this one, found on a side road on hill behind concentrator. This was a substantial building with one large and two smaller rooms upstairs, seven rooms downstairs, as well as a cellar, attic and large verandah. (Inset) The remains of an old stove in Alamo's garbage dump.*
*(Below) A general view of Sandon c1898.*
*(Bottom) Sandon, 60 days after the destructive fire of 1900.*

less profitable mines were closed. Conditions were better in the Slocan in 1923 than they had been for a number of years, and Sandon once again took on an air of prosperity. Old buildings were painted to look like new and every house and shack in the famous old camp became occupied. The Slocan Star, owned and operated by Silversmith Mines Limited, was the largest producer of silver-lead-zinc ore in the province, with the exception of the Sullivan mine in East Kootenay. Operations were continuous during the year, giving employment to an average of 98 men. During 1923 there were 37,895 tons of ore mined, yielding 100 ounces of silver per ton.

By 1930, because of declining silver prices, Sandon had again fallen on bad times. Earlier that year nearly all the producing mines had drastically curtailed operations or shut down completely, and Sandon was already becoming known as a ghost town. From 1941 until 1945 the town received a new lease on life when about 1,200 Japanese-Canadians were interned in the old buildings. Most of these people left at the end of the war to return to the coast. A few of the older ones stayed on, tending their small gardens and living out their remaining days in the tranquil setting, free from post-war bigotry.

In 1951-52 silver prices were increasing and a small mining boom occurred. Houses were fully occupied as some 1,000 people moved in. The town appeared to prosper once again but, alas, the boom was short-lived. When, on December 6, 1953, J.M. Harris, the man more closely associated with Sandon than any other, died in the New Denver Hospital at the age of 88, an era had ended.

In 1955 disaster struck again. Much snow had fallen during the winter; spring was late. Then rain was followed by extremely hot weather. High run-offs turned Carpenter Creek, which flowed under the boardwalk of Sandon's main street, into a raging torrent. It was not long before logs, boulders and other debris clogged the entrance to the flume and created a dam. Finally the pressure was too great and, with a tremendous roar, the rotting boardwalk was blasted away and raging waters tore through Sandon's main street. Some buildings were washed away immediately, while others were undermined and collapsed later. Railroad tracks were torn up and trestles washed away. Although its post office did not close until August 20, 1962, Sandon, as a town, was no more.

The population dwindled until only one permanent resident remained — Eugene Peterson, who had lived there for more than 50 years. He worked the old Victor mine on a lease basis from Dickenson Mines and made a comfortable living. Peterson, who was affectionately known throughout the district as the "Mayor" of Sandon, passed away in December, 1988.

Of the thousands of men and women who sought their fortunes at Sandon, a few struck it rich and were able to return home to enjoy the fruits of their labour. Most wound up toiling for wealthy mining companies. Many died in poverty, or came to an untimely end at Sandon.

Although the cemetery, about a mile below town, is overgrown with trees and brush and has almost disappeared, one can still see traces of unmarked graves, including those of a couple of infants who were probably victims of childhood diseases. On the few weather-beaten grave markers that do remain, most are inscribed with the letters, "W.F. of M." These initials stand for the Western Federation of Miners Union which was very powerful in Sandon in the late 1890s and early 1900s, and which provided the markers for burial of union members. The union was responsible for the large opera house, community hall, gymnasium and library in the Miners' Union Block in Sandon. They also owned the large hospital there — one of the few such hospitals in North America at that time.

Although the names on the markers are almost obliterated one can, with a little research, learn something of their tragic history. One was George Chapman, an elderly man who made a meagre living in the cleaning and pressing business, and supplemented his small income by the breeding and sale of canaries. Late one night fire broke out in his living quarters over a furniture warehouse. Old George was not found until after the fire was brought under control; he must have been a heavy sleeper as the charred remains were still reclined in the old-fashioned iron bedstead.

Markers which are still readable bear the names of two miners, Alex McFarlane, aged 30, and F.H. Sheppard, aged 28. The men were employed at the Noble Five mine, two miles above Sandon. On Thursday morning, March 8, 1900, they were returning home from the night shift accompanied by fellow worker Charles McNeil when they were overtaken by an avalanche. Volunteers from Sandon and surrounding mines were soon on the scene and were able to save McNeil; but they were too late for McFarlane and Sheppard.

Over the years souvenir hunters and vandals had stripped Sandon's last few buildings of anything of value. In search of old coins and artifacts of various kinds, floors, walls, and ceilings had been ripped apart. Light fixtures, intricately carved wooden staircase railings and bannisters had been carried away or wantonly destroyed. Natural decay has also taken a heavy toll.

In 1968, Hal Wright, an 11-year-old boy from Saltspring Island, went to visit his maternal grandmother in Nelson. Knowing that he was very interested in history, she took him to see Sandon — a visit that was eventually to bring new life to the old town.

By the time he returned home, Wright had already determined that he would do something about the town and its surroundings. He read books, magazine articles, visited museums, and wrote to the B.C. archives for old newspaper copies and photographs. For the next two or three years he visited his grandmother — and Sandon — whenever he could. He also began to collect photographs, artifacts, and other items with the idea of returning to Sandon to start a small museum and see what he could do to stem the decay, stop the vandalism, and shore up some of the old buildings. So enthusiastic himself, he quickened the interest of one of his schoolmates.

In 1972, Wright and his friend Steven Anderson decided to apply for an Opportunity for Youth grant to spend the summer in Sandon. They were given permission to use the old railway station and turn it into a museum. They also started to repair some of the old buildings, re-roof others and make some of the cabins habitable. Many tourists visited the area and some stayed on to help with the work. At the end of the summer most of the people returned to their homes and school, but Wright decided to remain in Sandon and to continue his schooling by correspondence. Thus Sandon gained another permanent resident.

During the long winter months, when not occupied with his school work, Wright took whatever work he could obtain that would enable him to continue buying tools and materials needed in the restoration work.

The museum soon outgrew its first home and permission was given to relocate

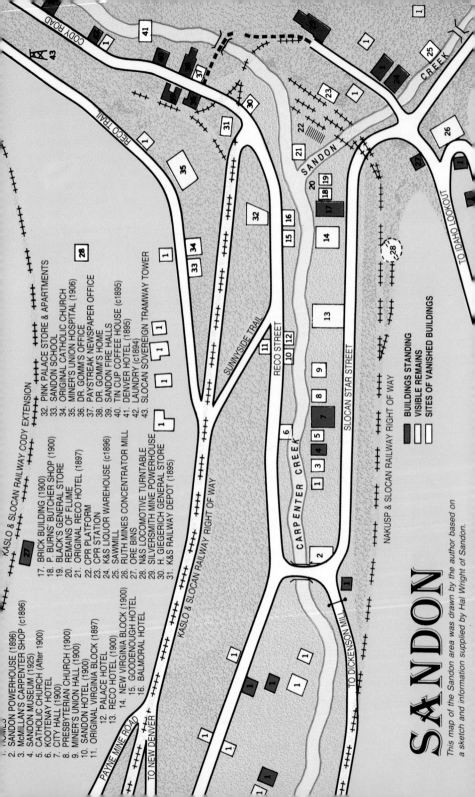

# SANDON

This map of the Sandon area was drawn by the author based on a sketch and information supplied by Hal Wright of Sandon.

2. SANDON POWERHOUSE (1896)
3. McMILLAN'S CARPENTER SHOP (c1896)
4. SANDON MUSEUM (1925)
5. CATHOLIC CHURCH (After 1900)
6. KOOTENAY HOTEL
7. CITY HALL (1900)
8. PRESBYTERIAN CHURCH (1900)
9. MINER'S UNION HALL (1900)
10. SANDON HOTEL (1900)
11. ORIGINAL VIRGINIA BLOCK (1897)
12. PALACE HOTEL
13. RECO HOTEL (1900)
14. NEW VIRGINIA BLOCK (1900)
15. GOODENOUGH HOTEL
16. BALMORAL HOTEL

17. BRICK BUILDING (1900)
18. P. BURNS BUTCHER SHOP (1900)
19. BLACK'S GENERAL STORE
20. REMAINS OF FLUME
21. ORIGINAL RECO HOTEL (1897)
22. CPR PLATFORM
23. CPR STATION
24. K&S LIQUOR WAREHOUSE (c1896)
25. SAWMILL
26. RUTH MINES CONCENTRATOR MILL
27. ORE BINS
28. N&S LOCOMOTIVE TURNTABLE
29. SILVERSMITH MINE POWERHOUSE
30. H. GIEGERICH GENERAL STORE
31. K&S RAILWAY DEPOT (1895)

32. PINK PALACE STORE & APARTMENTS
33. SANDON SCHOOL
34. ORIGINAL CATHOLIC CHURCH
35. MINER'S UNION HOSPITAL (1906)
36. DR. GOMM'S OFFICE
37. PAYSTREAK NEWSPAPER OFFICE
38. DR. GOMM'S HOME
39. SANDON FIRE HALLS
40. TIN CUP COFFEE HOUSE (c1895)
41. DENVER HOTEL (1895)
42. LAUNDRY (c1894)
43. SLOCAN SOVEREIGN TRAMWAY TOWER

BUILDINGS STANDING
VISIBLE REMAINS
SITES OF VANISHED BUILDINGS

KASLO & SLOCAN RAILWAY CODY EXTENSION

KASLO & SLOCAN RAILWAY RIGHT OF WAY

NAKUSP & SLOCAN RAILWAY RIGHT OF WAY

CARPENTER CREEK

RECO STREET

SLOCAN STAR STREET

SUNNYSIDE TRAIL

RECO TRAIL

CODY ROAD

CREEK

SANDON

TO IDAHO LOOKOUT

TO DICKENSON MILL

TO NEW DENVER

PAYNE MINE ROAD

*Sandon after the disastrous flood of 1955.*

it in the old policeman's house which subsequently was restored. At one time the provincial government seriously considered taking over the museum, but upon the change of government in 1975, the idea was dropped — at least for the time being. It is still being run on a voluntary basis during the summer by local residents. The mine is employing more workers now and slowly, but surely, the number of permanent residents is growing.

At the age of 19, Wright married Irene Palmer from neighbouring New Denver. Two years later their young daughter was born — another Sandon resident. Today the Wrights have three children: Jocelyn, Andrew and Annette, ages 11, 10 and 7. Along with Diane Wilkenson, who arrived from Calgary three years ago and now runs the coffee shop, and Veronika Pellowski who runs the museum, Sandon's current population stands at seven people and seven cats.

Although not much remains of Sandon as it was in its heyday — when it was known as the "Silver City" — the memories of its very colourful past are being kept alive. Wright estimates that more than 40,000 tourists a year visit Sandon and is pleased that the B.C. Heritage Trust is finally showing more interest in the old town-site. The Sandon Historical Society plans to restore the old brick general store, a project expected to cost $300,000. As well, plans are underway to ultimately restore the City Hall, and it is hoped a few key buildings might be rebuilt by private sponsors. Certainly Sandon, like Fort Steele and Barkerville, played an important enough role in the history of B.C. not to be left to rot in obscurity.

As for Three Forks, New Duluth and Cody, they have also disappeared. The fortunes of Three Forks were linked to the N&S. From the moment that railway completed its extension to Sandon, Three Forks began to fade. The day following Sandon's disastrous fire in May, 1900, the William Hunter Company of Three Forks wrote a letter to Mayor Pitts of Sandon stating: "There are lots of empty buildings down here and we will do all possible to put up any who wish to come down."

In 1904, the *Minister of Mines* reported that Three Forks was deserted, except for a few people who had local interest which still kept them there. The report concluded that a number of small rich properties "again gives promise of renewed mining activity in the vicinity, and of a new vitality to the old town, which, even now, can boast of two hotels and a store." By this time the population stood at about 100. Five years later, when the post office closed temporarily, Three Forks was all but finished. In 1916, mainly due to renewed mining activity in the area, Three Forks enjoyed a brief revival. But when its post office closed for good on August 31, 1921, there were only a handful of residents to mourn its passing. Today, not a single building remains.

New Duluth, a mile down the track, never amounted to much. During the summer of 1896 the Idaho-Alamo properties passed into the control of the Scottish Colonial Gold Fields Ltd. In June, 1897, the concentrator had "some radical changes made." That same year, Nathaniel Moore, the driving force behind the concentrator, passed away in Spokane.

Exactly when the siding came to be known as Alamo is not certain. Early newspapers always referred to it as New Duluth. However, when a post office was established there on April 1, 1899, the name Alamo was used. The post office closed on September 30, 1909.

In 1916 Alex McGillveray and Alex Millan were doing lease work on the Queen Bess property in the nearby mountains. When they got discouraged and gave up, Clarence Cunningham, acting for New York capital, took over the Alamo-Idaho, Queen Bess and Van-Roi groups. Cunningham had only extended the crosscut about 30 feet in the Queen Bess when he uncovered the famous bonanza that would yield $1,250,000 and earn him the nickname "lucky" for the rest of his life.

The following year Cunningham constructed an aerial tramway to transport the ore from these mines to the railway at Alamo and, with the returns from the Queen Bess ore, began construction of a new mill. By 1918, Cunningham was employing about 250 men at the Idaho-Alamo, Sovereign, Wonderful, Van-Roi, Hewitt and Wakefield, and the *Minister of Mines* gave him much of the credit for stimulating the resurgence in mining in the Slocan during this time. The next year, on August 1, 1919, the Alamo post office was reopened. Despite the fortune he took out of the mines, when Cunningham died in 1938 he was so deeply in debt that it took 11 years to untangle the legal details. The Alamo post office closed for good on August 4, 1939, and the small community was soon deserted.

Today, Alamo, unknown to many, still has a few buildings standing. Although the concentrator and nearby buildings are nothing but a pile of rubble, across the right of way are the remains of some two story buildings, one of which may have been the Queens Hotel. Over the hill behind the concentrator ruins, is the remains of a log building that once served as a stable. East of this location, on a flat area, are the remains of foundations and an enormous, well preserved building.

Cody, which once had visions of surpassing Sandon in size and stature, never had a population of over 150. By the time its post office closed on October 31, 1901, the town's days were numbered. It managed to hang on, just barely, for a few more years, but by 1910 it lay deserted. Today, the remains of the Noble Five concentrator and office can still be seen, along with debris from a couple of buildings and one residence. All other signs of activity have disappeared. The Silvery Slocan is quiet once more.

♣

# 8
# THE Ss *MOYIE*

*It is ironic that the* Moyie, *which was to serve the communities on Kootenay Lake for 59 years, was never intended for that location. She and her sister ship* Minto *were commissioned for the transportation of passengers and freight on the Stikine Route to the Klondike goldfields.*

IN 1897 the word "Klondike" had driven the world into a gold-hungry frenzy. From all over North America and Europe adventurers were heading for the Pacific coast. There, every manner of craft, whether seaworthy or not, was pressed into service transporting hordes of hopeful miners north. Most travelled by ship to Skagway or Dyea, disembarked, and climbed over the mountain passes. But there were several other routes to the goldfields as well.

One, which was heavily advertised by the merchants of Victoria and Vancouver as the only practical route, was via the Stikine River. This route held much promise for Canadians because it circumvented the U.S. customs at Skagway. Clifford Sifton, the Canadian Minister of the Interior, had travelled this "all-Canadian" route in the autumn of 1897 and had given it his approval. Envisioning that a wagon road, railway and steamboat line could complete the route, he signed a tentative contract with railway builders Sir William Mackenzie and Sir Donald Mann on January 26, 1898.

Superintendent Duchesnay of the Canadian Pacific Railway (CPR) had made a preliminary survey of the route in the fall of 1897 and had recommended a fleet of 12 sternwheelers be constructed for the river section. Hoping to grab a huge portion of the freight and passenger service, the CPR accepted his recommendation and awarded contracts for the steamers. Four were to be constructed at Port Blakely, Washington; five at False Creek, in Vancouver, and the remaining three in Toronto. Except for the three in Toronto, all were to be wooden-hulled.

The Betram Iron Works of Toronto was awarded the contracts for the construction of the *Moyie* and *Minto's* hulls. By having the prefabricated components manufactured in Toronto and shipped by rail to the coast, the CPR hoped to speed construction and have the vessels ready for the opening of summer traffic in 1898. Although the bottoms were to be planked in wood, the steel sides and bows made them much stronger and less susceptible to damage from ice, features which contributed greatly to the longevity of each of these two sternwheelers. The upper works and cabins were to be constructed at the assembly yards on the British Columbia coast.

The prefabricated components of the *Minto* and *Moyie,* each in 1,000 pieces, were shipped to the coast as planned. However, before any assembly could be

*(Above) This view of the* Moyie *backing away from the dock was probably taken at Kaslo.*

*(Opposite page) This painting, by B.C. artist Bill Maximick, depicts the* Moyie *churning up Kootenay Lake en route to Kaslo.*

*(Below) Freight like this was typical of what was carried by the* Moyie *during its heyday. As more efficient means of transportation were developed, however, revenues declined and the stern-wheelers gradually became obsolete.*

undertaken, prospects for the all-Canadian route to the Klondike turned sour. Materials for the railway had been delivered and Mackenzie and Mann had surveyed the route, 12 miles of which had actually been graded. But the Canadian Senate could not stomach the 4,000,000-acre land grant demanded by the railway builders, and refused to pass the appropriation. The CPR, meanwhile, in anticipation of the project proceeding, had heavily advertised the route and sold thousands of tickets. But when the unfortunate ticket holders arrived, there was no railway, only a rutted trail that even horses had trouble negotiating.

With the collapse of the Stikine Route, the CPR had to make alternate plans for its new vessels, only four of which actually saw limited service on the Stikine. The *Moyie* and *Minto* were diverted to the Kootenays. For this new service it was decided to lengthen the hulls of each by 20 feet. Even with this extension, however, the vessels were not large.

The *Moyie's* components arrived at Nelson late in June, 1898, where a crew of riveters began assembling the frames and steel plating. This work was completed in about a month and, on July 26, the riveters left Nelson for Nakusp to begin work on the *Minto.* Once the *Moyie's* hull had been assembled, carpenters, pipe fitters and painters took over. Finally, four months after its components had reached Nelson, the *Moyie* had been completed at a cost of $41,275. Like her sister ship *Minto,* she was 161 feet long (excluding the paddlewheel), 30 feet wide and five feet deep. Her engines, each with a single high-pressure cylinder 16 inches in diameter with a stroke of 72 inches, were capable of developing a total nominal horsepower of 17.

Box-like in appearance, the *Moyie* was licensed to carry 250 passengers with freight, 400 without. Minor differences made in each vessel resulted in the gross tonnage of the *Moyie,* at 835, being six more that the *Minto.*

In its issue of October 8, the Sandon *Mining Review* gave a brief description of the *Moyie:* "The smoking room is 48 feet long; the dining room 27½ feet; and the ladies cabin 40 feet. There are six staterooms which are being fitted up in first-class style. The bar is situated on the port side forwards, and on the same side are the toilet rooms and the linen room. On the starboard side are the purser's office and room and the steward's room. On the upper deck are two rooms on each side of the officers and a large room for the waiters."

On Saturday, October 22, 1898, a large crowd of excited spectators and dignitaries gathered at the CPR dock at Nelson awaiting the launch of the *Moyie.* A reporter for the Nelson *Miner,* who attended the event, wrote: "Mrs. Troup broke a bottle of champagne over the bow in the most approved fashion, the ropes were cut, the newly christened *Moyie* slid rapidly and safely down the ways, and, in much less time than it takes to write it, she was slowly and gracefully on the water with her steam up and everything ready for her trial trip."

Mrs. Troup was then presented with a cake basket by Chief Engineer Sproat on behalf of the shipyard workers. Then, with Captain Troup at the wheel, the *Moyie* circled around before returning to shore accompanied by the *Kokanee.* "About an hour afterwards," continued the *Miner,* "the steamer made a trial run up to 5-Mile Point and gave every satisfaction to those in charge of her. She is not quite as fast as the *Kokanee* but she can

*(Right) The* Moyie *undergoing renovations which included realignment of the superstructure, installation of a fire protection program, replacement of rotten wood, and re-canvassing the weather decks.*

*(Below) A view of the* Moyie *on the beach at Kaslo. This photo was taken in 1985, long before any restoration plans had commenced. (Inset) the Historic Sites and Monuments Board of Canada commemorative plaque at Kaslo.*

make 16 knots an hour."

After a successful trial run, the *Moyie* was brought back to Nelson where considerable work remained to be done on her passenger accommodations. The CPR planned to have her first official run coincide with a special excursion marking the opening of the Crowsnest railway line to Kootenay Landing, which was scheduled for December 6, 1898.

Dignitaries and invited guests from the communities of Rossland, Trail, Nelson, Kaslo and Sandon, among others, boarded the *Moyie* at Nelson at 8 a.m. on December 6. A half hour later she slipped from the dock on her historic journey. Upon arrival at Kootenay Landing, the dignitaries were served lunch on board.

Thus began the *Moyie's* long career of inaugurating passenger service between two railheads, the newly-opened Crowsnest line, which extended as far west as Kootenay Lake, and the Columbia & Kootenay Railway, which had its eastern terminus at Nelson. Service on the Crow run began with a timetable that called for a return trip from Nelson to Kootenay Landing each day. Connection with the Crow boat at Nelson was made in the chilly blackness of the early morning. As one traveller recalled:

"About 20 minutes past one o'clock we were rudely awakened from a sleep by jerks that almost shot us out of our berths. Our first thought. . .was that another accident had happened, but it proved to be nothing worse than the engine coupling on to take us down to the steamer. Once on board, some of the passengers lie down in the saloon and go to sleep then and there, others pay a dollar for a berth, but not without protesting that only half a dollar is due, and the night is half gone."

The steamer trip, while uneventful, was most enjoyable. Outside, the passing scenery changed at every turn, while inside the lounges were comfortable and the meals in the dining saloon, served by white-jacketed stewards, was a pleasant surprise. Another traveller wrote:

"We have never previously dined in the midst of such a lavish display of utensils and rich fare. . .which down to the fingerbowls themselves ranked first class. At dinner it was noticed that there are no class distinctions, one feature of the West which seemed more pronounced than ever. There are those whom fate has treated kindly and those to whom she has been a fickle jade."

Upon entering regular service, the *Moyie* took over from the overworked *Nelson*. Initially, the route was to Kuskanook, but with the opening of the Crowsnest line to passenger service, soon after the special excursion, the terminal was changed to Kootenay Landing. At first, traffic was light and the *Moyie's* accommodations were more than adequate. For many years she remained the regular steamer, linking the CPR's main east-west route through southeastern British Columbia. But by 1905, it was becoming clear that a larger, faster steamer would soon be needed to handle the heavy traffic. With the completion of the *Kuskanook*, in 1906, the *Moyie* was relegated to calling at the smaller landings to ease the schedule on the main line route.

Without a regular run of her own, the *Moyie* performed a variety of duties. She pushed railcar barges to various points around the lake, ran a biweekly service from Nelson to Gray Creek and Crawford Bay and, when needed, would relieve one of the steamers on their regular express runs. Performing these duties, together with her relatively slow speed and utilitarian appearance, when compared to the other faster, more graceful express steamers, earned her the title of "tramp boat."

Yet, ironically, it was these same unappealing features which made her, in the eyes of the CPR, "absolutely necessary to have available. . ." and why she was to outlive her other sisters by nearly three more decades.

But the *Moyie* was more than a mere work boat. Every Wednesday afternoon during the summer she would cast off from the Nelson wharf crowded with excursionists. Arrayed in their best holiday attire, they were bound for the hot springs at Ainsworth or the picnic grounds at the Outlet Hotel at Procter. Michael Cone describes these happy occasions:

"The most remembered outings during the summer months were the Sunday school picnics. For these festive outings, most often to Procter, the *Moyie* was usually made available for charter. The day would begin for the happy crowd of youngsters and parents with a leisurely trip up the West Arm. As the kids scurried around the decks, the older folk enjoyed quiet promenades or relaxed in deck chairs.

"Once the dock at Procter was reached, everyone would disembark and head for the grounds of the old Outlet Hotel. The young ones would run ahead to the large lawns and the adults would look for a nice spot for a picnic under the shade of the tall cottonwood trees.

"The rest of the day would be full of sporting activities and games, like sack races, football games and diving and swimming contests. And, best of all, there were big kegs of ice cream packed in salted ice and plenty of peanut and candy scrambles.

"At dusk a tired crowd would troop aboard the 'picnic' boat. The trip home though, was far from quiet. Usually there was a group singsong in the forward cabin and out on the decks. Sometimes a band was carried on board, and when the music started the tables and chairs in the dining saloon were cleared aside for an evening of dancing."

The steel sheathing on the sides of the *Moyie's* hull made her a handy vessel for shore landings and battling ice. Two fires on the beach or two flags being waved would bring the *Moyie* around and draw her toward shore — three fires, three flags or three shots from a rifle would signal an emergency. Just as her bow nudged into the beach, deck-hands would wrestle a long, narrow gangplank over the side and onto the shore. For a prospector accustomed to crossing creeks on a log, he had little trouble walking the springy plank as it swung and bounced up and down with his every step, but for the unwary tenderfoot it was much more difficult, although there was always an obliging, courteous mate or deck-hand standing nearby to offer a hand.

Ice created a real problem for the wooden-hulled steamers. The steel sheathing on the *Moyie's* hull offered greater protection, but there was always the danger of ice tearing the sheathing along the water-line. Because of this, breaking thick ice was usually done with either a railcar barge or an ice-breaking barge which was secured to the *Moyie's* bow. Michael Cone describes the procedure:

"Clearing a channel was slow going and meant long, hard hours of steady steaming. As the barge was pushed up on the ice, its stern would force the *Moyie's* bow down, at the same time lifting her paddle wheel almost out of the water.

"Once the weight of the barge had crushed the ice beneath it, then the barge's stern would suddenly rise, lifting the *Moyie's* bow with it and causing the paddle wheel to settle back into the water. As the big wheel cut deep into the water, the *Moyie* would move ahead and once again push the barge up onto the ice."

With the commencement of the First World War, lack of business brought the heyday of B.C. sternwheelers to a close. Some ceased operating altogether, while several were relegated only to summer service. Trade increased dramatically after the war, but now it was more than the sternwheelers were able to handle. As the network of railroads and highways spread further and further afield, siphoning off business, the use of steamers was becoming redundant.

By 1930, the CPR had substantially curtailed its passenger and railcar barge service on Kootenay Lake. This marked the end of over three decades of "main line" service between Nelson or Proctor and Kootenay Landing. One by one the steamers and tugs in the fleet were scrapped or sold. Robert Turner, in *Sternwheelers and Steam Tugs*, describes the end:

"At the same time, the *Kuskanook's* tri-weekly service from Nelson to Kaslo was terminated leaving only the *Moyie's* route from Procter to Crawford Bay, Lardeau and Kaslo as the one remaining sternwheeler service on Kootenay Lake.

"The sternwheelers and tugs were tied up at Procter to await their fates. The *Kuskanook* was permitted a brief reprieve, relieving the *Moyie,* which was given an overhaul, but after that was withdrawn. Despite being younger than the *Moyie,* the *Kuskanook* was the steamer considered surplus because of her wooden hull. She was sold in 1931."

By 1935, only the *Moyie* and *Granthall* remained. Sternwheelers *Nelson, Kokanee, International, Kaslo* and *Kuskanook* became only memories. The *Nasookin* enjoyed a brief reprieve. Purchased by the B.C. government to be used as an automobile ferry in 1933, she served in that capacity until 1947.

The *Moyie* continued to enjoy a happy and close association with all the communities and settlements along the lake, especially the ones that were still isolated and not easily accessible by road. For those places, many with not even a wharf to land at, the pattern and timetable of life beat to the rhythm of the *Moyie's* paddlewheel. Her regular arrival was a time for all to meet and talk with old friends, greet someone returning home, bid someone farewell, or simply pick up your mail.

But by the early 1950s, even the *Moyie* was beginning to show signs of her old age. Worst, her service record indicated that she was no longer paying her own way. Over the years rail traffic on the lake had dropped off noticeably, most of the cargo now being handled by freight and bus lines. In addition, people were preferring to drive in their cars rather than ride on the old boat. "In the face of these changes," wrote Michael Cone, "the *Moyie's* usefullness began to decline and there was little effort on the part of the CPR to maintain the traditional standards of service and comfort that had come to be accepted with steamer travel on the lake."

When her sister ship, the *Minto,* was retired in 1954, the *Moyie* remained the only active member of the once large fleet of sternwheelers. But it was clear that her time was also running out. The CPR, facing increasingly high maintenance costs and declining traffic, had no option but to retire its last sternwheeler. In March, 1957, they announced that the *Moyie's* last run would be made on April 27, 1957, bringing to an end 59 years of service.

As the *Moyie* slid from her dock at Proctor on that fateful Saturday morning in April, it was a sad day for residents of Kootenay Lake. As she had done numerous times before, her last regularly scheduled run would take her on an 87-mile trip to such familiar places as Queen's Bay, Kootenay Landing, Walker's Landing, Riondel, Ainsworth, Mirror Lake, Kaslo, Johnson's Landing, Lardeau and Argenta.

For long-term residents of the region this final sailing was particularly sad, and as she stopped at each community people turned out for a final farewell. At Lardeau a banner read "Farewell *Moyie*," and as she pulled from the dock she was given a horn-blowing sendoff by about 20 cars and trucks that had assembled for that purpose. The residents of Argenta presented the *Moyie* with a decorated wreath and as she left the strains of *Ould Lang Syne* followed her foaming wake. A daffodil

*(Above) The* International *and* Moyie *racing up Kootenay Lake.*
*(Below) Cords of wood such as this were stacked and used as fuel.*

wreath was presented at Johnson's Landing. At Kaslo, the largest community on the *Moyie's* route, the pilings of the dock were decorated with red, white and blue bunting and a large sign read: 'Better Lo'ed Ye Ne'er Be. Will Ye No Come Back Again.' Stores were closed, uniformed Boy Scouts stood at attention, volunteer fire fighters were on hand and a band played. Captain McLeod was presented with a photograph of his steamer, signed by the crew and many of the 100 passengers on board.

During her nine-hour voyage the *Moyie* called at 13 communities and everywhere the reception was warm and sad. Capt. G.A. West, of Shutty Beach, boarded her carrying three dozen daffodils for the passengers as he and his wife had always done for the past 38 years on their spring trip up the lake. Andrew Scott, aged 89, who had been at her Nelson launching, was on board as were many other long-time residents of the area. When she was tied up to the wharf at Procter late in the afternoon, the end to CPR sternwheeler service had come.

Fortunately, for posterity, the *Moyie* did not suffer the indignity of her sister, the *Minto,* which, in August of 1968, was towed to the centre of Upper Arrow Lake opposite Nakusp and set ablaze. Three years prior to the *Moyie's* retirement, upon rumours that she was nearing the end of her service, Jack Morris, president of the Kaslo Board of Trade, had written to G.A. Phillips, the CPR Superintendent at Nelson, expressing the desire of Kaslo to purchase the vessel and turn it into a museum. Phillips replied that he would keep them in mind upon the *Moyie's* retirement.

In February, 1957, word was received that the *Moyie* was to be retired the following April. When this news became public a few days later, the Nelson Junior Chamber of Commerce started a campaign to have the *Moyie* berthed at Lakeside Park in Nelson as a dance hall and coffee shop.

The CPR had stated publicly that the ship would go to the group showing they had the finances and ability to preserve her. Realizing the size of such an undertaking, the Kootenay Lake Historical Society (KLHS) was formed with Noel Bacchus, a trapper and rancher who had forsaken a London banking career for the freedom of Kootenay Lake, its first president. He contacted Victoria for a grant. A few days later, Premier W.A.C. Bennett phoned Morris asking if residents of Kaslo would be prepared to raise part of the $10,000 they said was needed. Morris replied that they would raise $2,500, and Bennett said he would then ask the House for the balance. On March 26, Morris received a telegram stating that the $7,500 grant had been approved. In addition, $1,810 had been raised through sale of memberships in the KLHS and a further $500 as a centennial grant. This information was forwarded to Phillips in Nelson.

On May 1, 1957, the CPR announced that the *Moyie* had been sold to the town of Kaslo "as is, where is" for $1. Sadly, a few days before arrangements could be made to have the *Moyie* towed to Kaslo, some CPR personnel pulled a boxcar alongside and began to strip her. Life rings, life jackets, water buckets, axes, toilets, sinks, hand basins, beds, springs, chairs, along with instruments from the pilot house and engine room were systematically removed. A few months later these items began to show up in second hand stores as collector's items. Someone had even removed sections of the Battleship linoleum. Fortunately, Morris and Bacchus found this hidden on shore and were able to have it re-laid on the main deck.

The *Moyie* was towed to Kaslo during high water and beached on the lake shore. To prepare a foundation, timbers from the high trestle bridge at Three Forks, which had been abandoned by the CPR, were purchased. These were laid on the beach and the *Moyie* was skidded into its present position. These timbers remained in place until 1988.

"Saving the *Moyie* from scrap was only the beginning of the continuing process of preserving the old vessel," wrote Robert Turner. "When she was retired, the *Moyie* was in generally good condition, but the CPR had not lavished excessive maintenance on a vessel of that age, due for retirement. Moreover, any vessel of predominantly wooden construction requires continuing maintenance. For the dedicated volunteers of the community, the painstaking task of keeping the *Moyie* sound began."

In 1978 the *Moyie* was declared a National Historic Site by Parks Canada. But, aside from a handsome plaque and $500 for refreshments at the plaque unveiling ceremony, nothing more was done. In 1981, $5,500 was contributed by Heritage Trust to fence the *Moyie* against vandalism. In 1983 Parks Canada surveyors examined the vessel and made a list of work necessary to preserve the ship, but by 1985 they had still not taken possession of the ship, and had only spent $10,000, mostly in interior clean-up and minor repairs, on her. Two years later, the Hon. Tom McMillan, Minister of the Environment, offered the KLHS a grant of $150,000 to $175,000 towards preservation, provided the KLHS could raise a similar amount. This seemed impossible for a small community with a population of 858.

Isabel Butler, a vice president of the KLHS and a past mayor of Kaslo, volunteered to head the fund-raising committee. Using mailing lists of Kaslo school graduates and former residents, and church socials, donations were received from more than a thousand individuals, organizations and companies. When the B.C. Lottery came through with a $100,000 grant in August, 1988, the Ss *Moyie* Preservation Fund had surpassed the $175,000 total it needed. Parks Canada presented the promised $175,000 and the KLHS hired a project manager for the $350,000 program.

Dick Smith, Kaslo's resident shipbuilder, provided the basic design for the steel crib to put the *Moyie* on the level again. Smith and his three man crew completed the job using 20 tons of steel and half a ton of welding rods in April, 1989, for $89,000 — $6,000 under budget. The other major components of the program included a new steel support crib, installation of a fire protection system, realignment of the superstructure, replacement of rotten wood, and re-canvassing the weather decks. Almost a mile of canvas, in 24-inch width, was bought.

The emergency phase ended in August, 1989, and has been followed by a $300,000 Phase II preservation program, scheduled for completion in August or September, 1990. In the meantime, B.C. Heritage Trust has recognized the *Moyie* as a B.C. Historic Landmark with a $250,000 grant. Part of this total ($90,000), is going into the Phase II preservation program and the rest will be used on the *Moyie* site and a visitor reception and interpretation centre, scheduled for completion in April, 1991.

In February, 1990, the Village of Kaslo, representing the people who have saved the *Moyie* as a remarkable heritage resource, received the highest honour the federal government can bestow: a Canadian Parks Service Heritage Award.

The KLHS is continuing its fund-raising efforts for complete restoration of the *Moyie,* with all the fittings and furnishings of the 1929-30 period. They, and all who have contributed to the preservation of this important piece of B.C. history are to be applauded for their efforts. ♣

# 9
# POPLAR CITY

*Most West Kootenay mining communities owed their existence to rich,*
*silver-producing mines. But Poplar City dreamed of golden wealth.*
*During its brief heyday, the town had seven hotels and a variety of*
*other businesses. Not to be outdone by Camborne, Ferguson or*
*Trout Lake City, it even had its own newspaper.*

EXCEPT for areas of clear-cut logging, the Lardeau and Duncan river valleys appear virtually as they did a century ago. Rugged mountain peaks, their heavily-timbered slopes carved by icy, swift-flowing creeks, provide a harsh but spectacular backdrop for pristine lakes and clear, unpolluted rivers. Not yet discovered by tourists, the area is today noted for fishing and lumbering.

The history of the region began in the 1880s when the first prospectors, searching for gold, reached the northern end of Kootenay Lake. Although the early efforts proved disappointing, the area continued to attract newcomers, and by the summer of 1891, the steam launch *Midge* was leaving Ainsworth every Wednesday for the Lardeau. Situated at the head of Kootenay Lake, the town of Lardo soon began to take shape. Soon a rough trail had been completed from the embryo town to the foot of Trout Lake. On December 11, 1892, the first 200 Lardo lots were offered for sale at $75 and $120. Within two weeks 150 had been purchased. When, on January 28, 1893, the remaining 50 had been sold, prices of new lots were increased to $100 and $160. By this time, as many as 300 men were encamped on the Duncan River waiting for the snow to melt. Unfortunately, most ran out of provisions and were forced to return to Lardo. By June a wharf had been completed and the town-site cleared, and Lardo became the main transportation centre for the region.

Meanwhile, prospectors were also drawn to the shores of Trout Lake where another mining rush, this one for silver, was gaining momentum. The first town-site to be established in this region was at Thompson's Landing (Beaton), which served as the gateway to the Lardeau mining district. Thompson's Landing was principally dependent upon transient traffic, as all freight destined for the mines came in that way. Located at the northern tip of Upper Arrow Lake, it was soon connected by a 12-mile wagon road to the head of Trout Lake. Along this road, three roadhouses, operated by Cook, Glenn and Beaty, had been established.

At the head of Trout Lake another new town soon began to take shape. By mid-February, 1893, lots in Trout Lake City were being offered for sale at $100 and $150. That spring, C.B. Hume arrived and began construction of a log general store, and by June, hotels, stores and private residences were also being built. A month later Andy Craig, manager for Hume's general store, reported that business was

*(Above) Logs float above what was once the site of Beaton.*
*(Left) The Beaton Hotel.*
*(Below) The historic Windsor Hotel in Trout Lake still stands and is still open for business.*

increasing steadily and kept "30 pack horses constantly on the trail between the town" and Thompson's Landing. In 1893 alone nearly 200 claims were staked in the nearby mountains.

"Prospecting in the Lardeau-Duncan was difficult," wrote Peter Chapman in *Where the Lardeau River Flows.* "Railroads and stern-wheelers brought prospectors to the northern and southern ends of the valleys but from there the going was arduous. Packhorse trails passed along the narrow valleys and clung to steep mountainsides as they ascended to the high country where most of the prospecting was done. The trail from Upper Arrow Lake to Trout Lake passed over an easy grade and caused no difficulty, but once the shores of Trout Lake were reached, the trails climbed steadily upwards into the mountains."

Two major railroad companies, the Canadian Pacific (CPR) and Great Northern, began to take an interest in the mining activity of the region, and in 1898 both began surveying the valleys. The CPR ultimately won the competition, and in 1899 construction was begun on a railway from Lardo. It followed the Lardeau River to Gerrard, at the foot of Trout Lake. The railroad grade provided easier access to the region, stimulated more prospecting, and in 1903 a rich strick was discovered near Poplar Creek.

On the morning of June 25, 1903, Frank Marquis and George Gilbert arrived in Kaslo with samples of quartz that was nearly half gold. The specimens were so incredible rich that if the entire mine were equally blessed, a figure of $100,000 a ton was considered low.

The properties where this rich find had been made were named the Gold Park and Ophir group, the two claims being located on Poplar Creek, a tributary of the Lardeau River, about 10 miles below Gerrard. Marquis and Gilbert had gone to town to obtain supplies, mortars and sacks for the ore. Naturally, their discovery created a great deal of interest in Kaslo as business men and miners gathered in excited groups to examine the rich specimens. By nightfall a number of parties had been organized and, utilizing whatever manner of craft that would float, departed for the goldfields. At Lardo, it was reported that anything that would roll on the rails was commandeered.

By July 2, a number of parties had returned to Kaslo. All verified the incredible richness of the strike. Their revelation that large quantities of platinum existed in the ore, as well as reports of rich placer finds, only served to further intensify the excitement and magnify the importance of the region.

In July, the *Trout Lake Topic* announced that three Trout Lake prospectors, O'Connor, Hamilton and Morgan, had made one of the largest discoveries yet in the camp. The three claims, the Lucky Jack, Lucky Three and Little Phil, were located only 800 feet from the Arrowhead & Kootenay (A&K) roadbed. Other rich claims were located in rapid succession as prospectors scrambled throughout the hills.

By this time, not surprisingly, Poplar Creek was the talk of the Kootenays and beyond, generating so much interest that the A&K decided to add extra coaches for a special excursion train on Sunday, August 9. Dignitaries, business men, prospectors and sightseers, entertained by an orchestra, rubbed shoulders on route to the rich goldfield. A mining superintendent was on board, and the Nelson *Daily News* even sent a reporter.

When they reached the mouth of Poplar Creek they were greeted by a sea of

***Frank Marquis and George Gilbert at their claim on Poplar Creek. It was their discovery
that caused a stampede into the area.***

canvas tents and hundreds of men clearing lots for buildings. The first building on
the site was a log cabin that had been build by Henry Magnusson three years
earlier. Elsewhere, what was to become the Pioneer Hotel was taking shape, and
within two weeks, two more hotels would be completed. Everywhere, small bush
fires roared as men cleared land for business and residential lots.

By the end of September, the litigation involving ownership of the town-site had
been resolved, and the real estate boom was on in earnest, its frenzy only controlled
through a lack of lumber. Although less than four months old, gambling had already
taken a strong hold, Jack Speirs, who had the contract for clearing Poplar's streets,
stating that "immense sums of money are being won and lost over the green cloth,
and all business houses have day and night shifts. Two trains are running on the
Kootenay and Arrowhead rail way, and with the music from the saloons and concert
halls, things are kept pretty lively both day and night."

By the end of October, Poplar City already boasted six of the seven hotels it
would support during its brief lifespan. Armstrong and Olmstrom's Poplar Hotel,
with 14 rooms, had been the first to be completed. It adjoined the A&K railway
station and boasted: "The wet grocery department contains pure goods, any brand
of which will produce optimistic results." The Kaiser House, also located convenient
to the railway depot, had 15 rooms and accommodation for 50 guests. Owner Fred
Kaiser advertised that "The nerve-bracer in the bar are free-milling, and an orchestra
provides music while the guests are at dinner." The Grand Hotel, owned by Jacobson

(Above) The remains of an old log cabin at the Poplar Creek town-site in 1990.
(Right) Col. Robert Lowery, probably the best newspaper editor of the Canadian frontier.
(Below) A view of Poplar Creek today. The town-site was located behind photographer to the right.

*(Top) The John Logus homestead.*
*(Above) John Keen.*
*(Right) Poplar Creek has only one full-time resident who lives just south of the old town-site. These horses belong to him.*
*(Below) J.J. Cameron built the first hotel in Poplar Creek.*

and Anderson, offered the best menu in the city and touted their 17 rooms as "large and comfortable." The Royal, owned by Charles Ehlers, contained 14 rooms and offered "cocktails for the nervous, beer for the delicate, whiskey for the hardy mountaineer, and cigars for those who prefer narcotic to alcoholic stimulants." The Dominion, owned by Hambly and Schmock, contained 18 rooms and set a "table supplied with the best in the market." Poplar's largest hotel, with 20 rooms, was the Miner's, owned by Hansen, Strand and Johnson.

By this time, a number of businesses had also been established. E.L. Masterson operated a general store that provided mining supplies, dry goods, clothing, hardware, boots, shoes and groceries. J.J. Cameron had sold his hotel in Lardo to move to Poplar where he sold groceries, provisions, hardware, tinware and canned goods, offering delivery to any part of the city. He also operated the post office. S.F. Peterson operated a restaurant. George Chattaway's Poplar Transfer Company had a heavy team of horses and a string of husky mules available for hire. Chattaway also owned a livery barn and a residence. There was also a hardware store operated by Archer and Hodder, two notaries, John Keen and Edward Bowie, a government record office and police office, an assay office, a "tourist retreat," other stores and offices, and numerous residences.

The citizens of Poplar were already considering incorporation under the speedy Incorporation of Towns Act, and were anxious to install their own water works and electric light plant without the intervention of private companies. The town, as a whole, had the vigorous appearance of a well-to-do camp, which indeed it was.

Amid all this prosperity, however, there was a sombre note permeating throughout the camp that would have far-reaching significance. In September, Ed Tanghe located and staked a placer claim called the Shamrock upon ground already staked by the Lucky Jack mineral claim. The question then arose, who owned the rights: the placer claim or the mineral claim?

On October 24 the Gold Commissioner inspected the placer claim and decided that it was endangering the workings of the Lucky Jack, and ordered Tanghe to move the stakes of the Shamrock. If he complied, the Shamrock would be on almost barren ground, so Tanghe decided to pursue the matter in the courts. In the meantime, however, he continued to work the claim, and on Thursday, November 5, he was arrested and charged with stealing ore from the Lucky Jack and with disobeying the lawful order of the Gold Commissioner.

After a long hearing at Trout Lake City, Tanghe was sent up for trial on the first charge, and sentenced to three months hard labour on the second. Tanghe's lawyer argued the charges should have been brought before a civil court, and said he had commenced action against Morgan, locator of the Lucky Jack, against Great Northern Mines, the present owner, and against Fred Fraser, the Gold Commissioner.

While this turmoil was simmering in the background, Poplar City faced a more immediate threat. On Saturday, October 30, the nemesis of all wooden, frontier towns, fire, was detected on the roof of the Poplar Hotel. Fortunately the fire occurred in the afternoon, was quickly detected and soon extinguished. Had it started during the night, most of the new town would probably have been destroyed. The cause of the fire turned out to be a defective flue pipe. Nearly all other buildings in town already had brick chimneys, and the Poplar Hotel owners vowed to construct one as quickly as possible.

On December 4, Poplar City grew somewhat in stature with the introduction of its own weekly newspaper, *The Nugget.* Published every Friday by Robert Lowery, the "Colonel of the Kootenays," who had or would publish papers in Nelson, Kaslo, Sandon, Nakusp, New Denver, Fernie and Greenwood, it provides us with valuable insights into the growth and death of a frontier community, which, by this time, had a population of about 300.

"As a rule we like to get into camp before the pianos and canary birds," editorialized Lowery in his first issue, "but on our arrival last week we found these things had preceded us, in addition to a large number of birds that are not canaries. The camp is a little over 100 days old and has six hotels, five of which are producing every day, four stores, a livery barn, a laundry, etc., and more gold in the hills around the burg than we have ever got close to since we first planted a set of stakes in the shadow of the grand old mountains of the Great West. No church as yet parts the air with its tall spire. . . ."

More pressing than a church was the community's need for a school. In its December 11 issue, *The Nugget* announced that a meeting had been held by citizens interested in establishing a school in Poplar. Four trustees had been elected, and a requisition forwarded to the superintendent of schools. On January 15, 1904, the paper proclaimed: "School will be opened next week in Poplar if the furniture arrives. J.J. Cameron is moving his school plant from Lardo here. Mr. Cameron is perhaps the only person in Canada who is the owner of a complete public school outfit. When the school opened in Lardo some years ago he put up the cost for all the necessary furniture. As he has never been reimbursed for his outlay, and as Lardo has about run out of population, he has decided to move his entire plant from Lardo to Poplar, where it will be run full time."

Despite this announcement, however, a public school for Poplar was still a long way off. Hopes were dashed in mid-February when David Wilson, the inspector for schools for Kootenay and Boundary visited Poplar and stated that there were only seven children of school age in the town, not a sufficient number to justify a school.

Despite this setback, the winter of 1903-04 was one of continued growth and activity for Poplar. Cold weather and snow had brought mining to a virtual standstill, and some of Poplar's residents and business men had gone out for the winter. But those who remained stayed active. In December, while the proprietors of the Dominion brought in materials to lath and plaster their hotel, Fred Kaiser began construction of a two-storey, 40x60-foot addition to his. Next door to the Royal, Jost and Ostby had erected the Poplar Meat Market and were ready for business by mid-December. Early in the same month *The Nugget* moved into its two-storey, 24x50-foot building that boasted 10-foot ceilings. As the new year approached, John Hambley's new store on Front Street opened for business. Yet, despite all this activity, the paper complained that construction was at a standstill because of a lack of lumber.

In January, the Poplar Barbershop opened in the Pioneer Hotel. The barber was Turk Brown, who soon purchased a building lot on Railroad Avenue for his residence. During this same time a couple of hotels changed hands. William Schmock sold his interest in the Dominion to J.N. Nelson, while A.O. Ostby purchased Oscar Johnson's interest in the Miner's Hotel, the name of which was then changed to the Hotel Inn. Later still, the Hotel Inn became the Commercial.

On January 29, the town experienced its first robbery when a thief broke into the Poplar Butcher Shop and stole a couple of hams, some bacon and porter-house steaks. A small amount of cash in the till was left undisturbed and the total robbery

(Above) An old piece of machinery at Gerrard.
(Right) This unidentified building stands across the Lardeau River from the original Gerrard town-site.

(Below) On the hill over-looking the main Gerrard town-site once stood a row of railway company houses. Today, the half dozen ruins that remain are the only visible sign of the old Arrowhead & Kootenay terminus.

amounted to less that $20, but that did not stop Lowery from launching a tirade at the thief. "No one in a mining camp need resort to theft in order to eat. There is always work in a new camp for a man who is willing to work. It is a very unusual occurrence in a mining camp, especially in a small place like Poplar, for a theft to be committed. We do not believe there is a business man in the camp who would refuse a person a chance to earn food. We would advise the thief to hit the road."

February proved to be another busy month: E. Harrop's store on Front Street was completed, a new addition to the Hotel Inn was finished, and the Harrop Block, promising to be the "handsomest building" in town, was nearing completion. In addition, a number of new residences had been or were being erected. All the businesses in town reported a busy month, particularly the hotels, because of a large transient trade.

Despite the fact that it was growing daily and its future appeared bright, Poplar

*(Right) A.G. "Joe Miser" Johnson on the steps of his store in Poplar Creek.*
*(Below) An early view of Poplar Creek. When this photo was taken the town-site was still tree-covered and the town was in its infancy. A year later it had boomed and busted.*

was still without a bank, prompting *The Nugget* to lament: "Poplar needs a bank. The citizens have grown tired depositing their money in snowbanks, and making drafts through the cracks in the wall of their domiciles." Despite repeated requests for a financial institution to locate in Poplar, however, none ever did.

If Poplar can be said to have had a heyday during its brief existence, the months of March, April and May, 1904, would be it. The snow was fast disappearing from the hills and the twice-weekly A&K trains were filled with prospectors and mining men returning for another season. Business men were also returning from wintering on the outside, and a flood of new entrepreneurs, gamblers and real estate boomers could be seen everywhere.

Speculators were now asking $1,000 for lots, and the original 20-acre flat upon which the town-site was located was soon filled. This prompted the town-site company to add an addition, which they called Findland Heights, on the east side of Poplar Creek.

E.L. Masterson was building a large storehouse, an addition to the Poplar Hotel was well underway and arrangements were being made for a dairy and contracts were let for numerous new residences. A sure sign that the town had arrived was the "Poplar Nugget," a new cigar manufactured specifically for Jacobson and Anderson's Grand Hotel.

The pace increased in April when three carloads of lumber arrived. McCallum's new store on Poplar Avenue was soon completed, as was Turk Brown's new barber-shop on Railroad Avenue. A week later Brown added a bathroom to the premises. During the same month F.C. Lawrence opened a watch and jewellery shop opposite the Grand Hotel. Poplar now also boasted a drug store, operated by Dr. Brandon of Trail, a blacksmith, Andy Garvey and two more barbershops. Plans were underway for May Day celebrations which were to include a baseball game in the park on Findland Heights and other games downtown. Prospects for the town appeared so bright, in fact, it prompted John Keen, one of the Poplar Townsite Company owners to state: "We expect to see three hundred houses up this year before the snow flies, and it will take that many to supply the demand."

Throughout its brief history, *The Nugget* continually provided details of new discoveries, such as on March 25: "Some of the richest ore yet found in camp is being taken out of the Swede group this week. No assay has been made, but the quartz is fully one-half gold, and will run $100,000 to the ton." Yet, despite all the reported richness of the various claims continually being discovered or worked on, one thing was become apparent, *no significant shipments of ore had been made.* This was partly due to the Lucky Jack-Shamrock litigation, still unresolved, which was beginning to cast doubts over the entire district. However, this was not the main consideration. It was gradually becoming clear that, although the mines around the town were surface wonders, the veins did not go to depth.

As one reads the pages of *The Nugget* for the summer and fall of 1904, it soon becomes evident that Poplar has reached its peak and was already starting to decline. The clues are almost imperceptible at first; in fact, new construction and additions to existing establishments continue throughout the decline. On May 13 *The Nugget* boasted that "Poplar is going ahead so fast that hotel extensions cannot keep up with the increasing trade."

In the short term, this may have appeared true. Certainly P.H. Carey still believed in the town's future when, in early June, he began construction on a two-storey,

*Four armed men, and what appears to be a young woman, with rifle, guard the Lucky Jack mineral claim in May, 1903.*

28x50-foot hotel. During the same month, E.E. Chipman, the government agent at Kaslo, arrived in town with plans for the new government block. The 20x30-foot building, in the first phase of construction, included a jail with accommodations for three prisoners and a two-room constable's office. On June 10, Mrs. J.J. Cameron gave birth to a 10-pound boy, the first person to be born in Poplar. By mid-June, S.F. McKay's long-awaited sawmill was up and running, and work had finally been started on the school. When the Grand Central opened for business on July 1, it was Poplar's seventh hotel. So, on the surface, everything appeared to be progressing nicely.

But subtle news items appearing in *The Nugget* painted a different scenario: George Chattaway had sole his draying business; the Royal Hotel had been sold to E.L. Morand; A.O. Ostby had sold the Poplar Meat Market to Tattrie & Chisholm; and Fred Kaiser had sold his interest in the Kaiser House to Henry Magnusson. Before the end of July, Mr. & Mrs. Cameron and family had left Poplar for Trail, where Mr. Cameron would engage in business.

By this time business had taken a definite downturn, prompting *The Nugget* to remark: "Although business does not appear to be very brisk in Poplar, eight pack animals are kept busy every day taking supplies to the mines and prospects on the different creeks in the vicinity of Poplar."

*The Nugget,* is appears, was putting on a brave front in the face of reality. Back in mid-April, during the town's peak, the newspaper had associated its increase in size from four pages to six with the town's prosperity. On August 5, however, the newspaper had dropped back down to four pages without similar fanfare. During the same month Jackson Radcliffe put his Poplar Laundry up for rent and left for Nelson.

Ironically, in the midst of this decline, Poplar finally got what it wanted most; a school, Miss Dickensen coming from Vancouver as the teacher. Another upbeat note was McKay's sawmill, which had produced 100,000 feet of lumber. It was working steadily and employed 12 people. But, once again, these were mixed signals. While it was true that the sawmill employed 12 people, one of its employees was Poplar's first barber, Turk Brown, who apparently could no longer earn a living trimming the beards of a vanishing breed of prospectors.

Unfortunately, despite brief glimmers of hope, there was no turning back the clock for Poplar, and on September 30 *The Nugget* lamented: "Railroad avenue is now a deserted place. Not even the red blinds are left." A month later the newspaper shut down and left. Lowery wrote: "This week *The Nugget,* editor, printer, pressman and devil, hies himself to the railroad track and takes a nearly southern course as the transportation companies have furnished. . . ."

For a time Poplar clung precariously to life, but its days were sadly numbered. McKay dismantled his sawmill and moved to Fernie, businesses closed and residents moved away. By the end of 1905 Poplar was virtually a true ghost town of false-fronted buildings haunted by a few die-hards. For decades, the gaunt, weather-beaten structures stared back at passengers passing by on the A&K trains on route to Gerrard. Gradually, however, the elements took their toll so that, one by one, the old buildings collapsed. Today, most of the signs of Poplar have disappeared. You can still find some gnarled apple trees, sunken foundations and piles of scattered debris here and there, and you can still wander among the abandoned workings of the Lucky Jack. But of Poplar City, the hell-raising town with the promising golden future, nothing remains but the memories.                                    ♣

# ACKNOWLEDGEMENTS

For the most part, this book was researched and written from the information contained in the various newspapers of the day. Previously published books were then used to tie up loose ends or fill in the gaps left by the local papers. The most important acknowledgement I can give, therefore, is to the publishers whose provided the many details and facts that could not have been obtained from any other source. A similar gratitude is offered to the pioneers themselves. Many were active in the history of not one, but several West Kootenay towns as new discoveries led them from region to region. Without their entrepreneurial and pioneering activities, there would be no history to write.

Finally, a special acknowledgement must be given to N.L. Barlee, whose two articles "Rossland: City of Gold" and "John Kirkup: Lawman of the West" were combined and edited to form the chapter "Rossland: The Golden City." Similarly, David Scott's article "Robert Sproule: Murderer or Martyre?" was merged and edited with Craig Weir's article "Bluebell: A Mining Saga" to form the chapter of the same name. The contribution of N.L. Barlee, David Scott and Craig Weir on these two chapters allowed the author to devote more time to researching and writing the remainder of the book.

# BIBLIOGRAPHY

NEWSPAPERS:

Ainsworth *Hot Spring News.*
Bonner's Ferry *Herald.*
Camborne *Miner.*
Ferguson *Lardeau Eagle.*
Kaslo *British Columbia News.*
Kaslo *Claim.*
Kaslo *Slocan Prospector.*
Kaslo *Kootenanian.*
Nakusp *Ledge.*
Nelson *Miner.*
Nelson *Daily Miner.*
Nelson *Daily News.*
Nelson *Economist.*
Nelson *Lowery's Claim.*
Nelson *Tribune.*

New Denver *Ledge.*
Poplar Creek *The Nugget.*
Sandon *Mining Review.*
Sandon *Paystreak.*
Sandon *Slocan Mining Record.*
Silverton *Silvertonian.*
Slocan City *Drill.*
Three Forks *Slocan Prospector.*
Trout Lake *Lardeau Mining Review.*
Trout Lake *Topic.*
Victoria *Colonist.*
Victoria *Times.*
Ymir *Mirror.*
Ymir *Herald.*

# BOOKS & PERIODICALS:

Barlee, N.L. *Best of Canada West #1.* Stagecoach Publishing, Langley, B.C., 1978.
————, *West Kootenay: Ghost Town Country.* Canada West Publications, 1984.
Blake, Don. *The Valley of the Ghosts.* Don Blake, 1988.
Brock, Prof. R.W. *Poplar Creek and Other Camps of the Lardeau District.* Journal of the Canadian Mining Institute, 1904.
Chapman, Peter. *Where the Lardeau River Flows.* Provincial Archives of B.C. Sound Heritage Series #12, 1981.
Graham, Clara. *Fur and Gold in the Kootenays.* Wrigley Printing Co., Vancouver, B.C., 1945.
Kaslo Board of Trade. *Kaslo, B.C. The Lucerne of North America.*
Lees, J.A. & Clutterbuck, W.J. *A Ramble in British Columbia.* Longmans, Green, and Co., London, England, 1888.
May, Dave. *Sandon: The Mining Centre of the Silvery Slocan.* Dave May, 1986.
Ringheim, Margery. *Historical Kaslo.* Kootenay Lake Historical Society, Kaslo, B.C., c1966.
Smyth, Fred J. *Tales of the Kootenays.* Douglas & McIntyre, Vancouver, B.C., 1977 reprint of 1937 edition.
Topping, William. *British Columbia Post Offices.* William Topping, 1983.
Turnbull, Elsie. *Ghost Towns and Drowned Towns of West Kootenay.* Heritage House Publishing, Surrey, B.C., 1988.
———— *Trail: A Smelter City.* Sunfire Publications, Langley, B.C., 1985.
*B.C. Historical Quarterly,* various issues.
*B.C. Mining Record,* various issues.
*B.C. Minister of Mines Report,* various issues.
*Poplar Creek Goldfields.* Pamphlet published by Nelson *Daily News,* Nelson, 1903.

# INDEX